OPPOSING
VIEWPOINTS®
SERIES

| Campaign Finance

Other Books of Related Interest

Opposing Viewpoints Series

The Democratic Party
The Fifth Estate: Extreme Viewpoints from Alternative Media
Identity Politics
Voting Rights
Western Democracy at Risk

At Issue Series

The Deep State
The Federal Budget and Government Spending
Gerrymandering and Voting Districts
Politicians on Social Media
Populism in the Digital Age

Current Controversies Series

Are There Two Americas?
Executive Orders
The Political Elite and Special Interests
Political Extremism in the United States
States' Rights and the Role of the Federal Government

"Congress shall make no law ... abridging the freedom of speech, or of the press."

First Amendment to the US Constitution

The basic foundation of our democracy is the First Amendment guarantee of freedom of expression. The Opposing Viewpoints series is dedicated to the concept of this basic freedom and the idea that it is more important to practice it than to enshrine it.

OPPOSING
VIEWPOINTS®
SERIES

Campaign Finance

Kathryn Roberts, Book Editor

GREENHAVEN
PUBLISHING

Published in 2019 by Greenhaven Publishing, LLC
353 3rd Avenue, Suite 255, New York, NY 10010

Articles in Greenhaven Publishing anthologies are often edited for length to meet page
requirements. In addition, original titles of these works are changed to clearly present
the main thesis and to explicitly indicate the author's opinion. Every effort is made to
ensure that Greenhaven Publishing accurately reflects the original intent of the authors.
Every effort has been made to trace the owners of the copyrighted material.

Cover image: HQuality/Shutterstock.com; HQuality/Shutterstock.com

Library of Congress Cataloging-in-Publication Data

Names: Roberts, Kathryn, 1990– compiling editor.
Title: Campaign finance / Kathryn Roberts, book editor.
Description: First Edition. | New York : Greenhaven Publishing LLC, 2019. |
  Series: Opposing Viewpoints | Includes bibliographical references and
  index. | Audience: Grades 9–12.
Identifiers: LCCN 2018023310| ISBN 9781534504110 (library bound) | ISBN
  9781534504332 (paperback)
Subjects: LCSH: Campaign funds—United States—Juvenile literature.
Classification: LCC JK1991 .C3424 2019 | DDC 324.7/80973—dc23
LC record available at https://lccn.loc.gov/2018023310

Manufactured in the United States of America

Website: http://greenhavenpublishing.com

Contents

Chapter 1: Are There Benefits to Publicly Financed Campaigns?

Chapter 2: Why Is Private Campaign Financing the Most Popular Way to Raise Funds?

Chapter 3: Do Corporate Donations Need More or Less Regulation?

Chapter 4: Why Is Transparency in Campaign Financing Important to Fair Elections?

The Importance of Opposing Viewpoints

Perhaps every generation experiences a period in time in which the populace seems especially polarized, starkly divided on the important issues of the day and gravitating toward the far ends of the political spectrum and away from a consensus-facilitating middle ground. The world that today's students are growing up in and that they will soon enter into as active and engaged citizens is deeply fragmented in just this way. Issues relating to terrorism, immigration, women's rights, minority rights, race relations, health care, taxation, wealth and poverty, the environment, policing, military intervention, the proper role of government—in some ways, perennial issues that are freshly and uniquely urgent and vital with each new generation—are currently roiling the world.

If we are to foster a knowledgeable, responsible, active, and engaged citizenry among today's youth, we must provide them with the intellectual, interpretive, and critical-thinking tools and experience necessary to make sense of the world around them and of the all-important debates and arguments that inform it. After all, the outcome of these debates will in large measure determine the future course, prospects, and outcomes of the world and its peoples, particularly its youth. If they are to become successful members of society and productive and informed citizens, students need to learn how to evaluate the strengths and weaknesses of someone else's arguments, how to sift fact from opinion and fallacy, and how to test the relative merits and validity of their own opinions against the known facts and the best possible available information. The landmark series Opposing Viewpoints has been providing students with just such critical-thinking skills and exposure to the debates surrounding society's most urgent contemporary issues for many years, and it continues to serve this essential role with undiminished commitment, care, and rigor.

The key to the series' success in achieving its goal of sharpening students' critical-thinking and analytic skills resides in its title—

Opposing Viewpoints. In every intriguing, compelling, and engaging volume of this series, readers are presented with the widest possible spectrum of distinct viewpoints, expert opinions, and informed argumentation and commentary, supplied by some of today's leading academics, thinkers, analysts, politicians, policy makers, economists, activists, change agents, and advocates. Every opinion and argument anthologized here is presented objectively and accorded respect. There is no editorializing in any introductory text or in the arrangement and order of the pieces. No piece is included as a "straw man," an easy ideological target for cheap point-scoring. As wide and inclusive a range of viewpoints as possible is offered, with no privileging of one particular political ideology or cultural perspective over another. It is left to each individual reader to evaluate the relative merits of each argument—as he or she sees it, and with the use of ever-growing critical-thinking skills—and grapple with his or her own assumptions, beliefs, and perspectives to determine how convincing or successful any given argument is and how the reader's own stance on the issue may be modified or altered in response to it.

This process is facilitated and supported by volume, chapter, and selection introductions that provide readers with the essential context they need to begin engaging with the spotlighted issues, with the debates surrounding them, and with their own perhaps shifting or nascent opinions on them. In addition, guided reading and discussion questions encourage readers to determine the authors' point of view and purpose, interrogate and analyze the various arguments and their rhetoric and structure, evaluate the arguments' strengths and weaknesses, test their claims against available facts and evidence, judge the validity of the reasoning, and bring into clearer, sharper focus the reader's own beliefs and conclusions and how they may differ from or align with those in the collection or those of their classmates.

Research has shown that reading comprehension skills improve dramatically when students are provided with compelling, intriguing, and relevant "discussable" texts. The subject matter of these collections could not be more compelling, intriguing, or urgently relevant to today's students and the world they are poised to inherit. The anthologized articles and the reading and discussion questions that are included with them also provide the basis for stimulating, lively, and passionate classroom debates. Students who are compelled to anticipate objections to their own argument and identify the flaws in those of an opponent read more carefully, think more critically, and steep themselves in relevant context, facts, and information more thoroughly. In short, using discussable text of the kind provided by every single volume in the Opposing Viewpoints series encourages close reading, facilitates reading comprehension, fosters research, strengthens critical thinking, and greatly enlivens and energizes classroom discussion and participation. The entire learning process is deepened, extended, and strengthened.

For all of these reasons, Opposing Viewpoints continues to be exactly the right resource at exactly the right time—when we most need to provide readers with the critical-thinking tools and skills that will not only serve them well in school but also in their careers and their daily lives as decision-making family members, community members, and citizens. This series encourages respectful engagement with and analysis of opposing viewpoints and fosters a resulting increase in the strength and rigor of one's own opinions and stances. As such, it helps make readers "future ready," and that readiness will pay rich dividends for the readers themselves, for the citizenry, for our society, and for the world at large.

Introduction

> *"A candidate with a large war chest of funds is seen as formidable. Campaign money can be a market-based signal of a candidate's viability. Likewise, a candidate with a small balance is seen as vulnerable or weak, or as having significant liabilities."*
>
> —*Jennifer Victor, Vox*

The United States government has endeavored to reconcile politics' intimate relationship with money to hotly-debated levels of success since Andrew Jackson launched his presidential campaign in 1828 through a political patronage system that was intended to reward political party operatives. It wasn't until the 1860s that the US Government first attempted to reign in campaign finance through the Naval Appropriations Bill of 1867. In the early 1900s, Congress passed the Tillman Act, which intended to prohibit corporations and national banks from directly providing funds to federal candidates. This law, named for South Carolina Senator Ben Tillman, established the framework for the United States' current laws regarding campaign finance.

The issue with these laws was that they were rarely ever enforced, deeming them largely ineffective. It was not until 1971 that Congress passed the Federal Election Campaign Act, intended to ensure transparency in federal campaigns through disclosure of funds, which means that the public can see who donates to which federal candidate or political party—to an extent. The law was further strengthened in 1974 when, following President Richard

Nixon's Watergate scandal, the FECA was amended to establish a comprehensive system of campaign finance regulation through the creation of the Federal Election Commission.

Though Congress has continued to strengthen campaign finance reform in the decades since, many laws passed over the years have been struck down by the Supreme Court as unconstitutional, primarily due to violations of peoples' First Amendment rights. These Supreme Court decisions come through lawsuits including *Buckley v. Valeo* in 1976, and most recently the case of *Citizens United v. Federal Election Commission* in 2010.

Ruled violations of US Citizens' First Amendment rights are one of the most common roadblocks for modern attempts and campaign finance reform, which is also seen in states that have public campaign finance laws in place, including Arizona, Connecticut, and Maine. That said, the rise in states with either public campaign finance laws or the option for candidates who run only through the acceptance of public funds show a rise not only in campaigns in which the incumbent does not run unopposed, but also gives rise to a more diverse pool of candidates, including women, minorities, and people who do not have the financial backing of the Hillary Clintons or Jeb Bushes of the world.

While there are laws in place that limit how much money a federal candidate is legally allowed to accept, the 2010 *Citizens United* decision created a significant loophole that has allowed millions upon millions upon millions of funds to be funneled into electoral campaigns through the creation of Political Action Committees, commonly known as PACs, and Super Political Action Committees, also known as *Super PACs*. Per the Supreme Court's 5-4 ruling in 2010, these organizations, specifically *Super PACs*, are not allowed to coordinate directly with the candidates they are created to support, which the courts define as not causing any conflicts of interests or candidate manipulation. Whether that is actually true remains to be seen, but these organizations have allowed recent elections to become some of the most expensive in the history of the United States. Some of that can be connection to normal inflation rates as the US economy expands, but the rest brings to question just how much an organization is willing to pay to "buy" a person's vote for their preferred candidate.

Opposing Viewpoints: Campaign Finance examines the recent and rapid changes in the United States' campaign finance laws and other related issues in chapters titled "Are There Benefits to Publicly Financed Campaigns?", "Why Is Private Campaign Financing the Most Popular Way To Raise Funds?", "Do Corporate Donations Need More or Less Legislation", and "Why Is Transparency in Campaign Financing Important to Fair Elections?" These questions delve into studies of race and wealth in the United States and pose a number of difficult-to-answer questions about just how much control the richest .05-percent of American citizens have over the United States' elections and the establishment of public policy.

Are There Benefits to Publicly Financed Campaigns?

Chapter Preface

In a heavily politicized American society in which federal campaigns are run through treasure chests filled with millions and millions of dollars—and seem to increase with each successive election cycle—at the state level, some states have successfully passed laws that allow for qualified candidates to run their campaigns on public funds. These states include Arizona, Connecticut and Maine, whose laws have mostly stood the test of many legal challenges.

One of the many challenges focuses on the laws passed in the state of Arizona, where the public campaign finance laws include a 10 percent surcharge on both criminal and civil fines to fund the program. In the case of *May v. McNally* in 2002, an Arizona legislator claimed that it would be against his First Amendment rights to pay that 10 percent fine he received on a parking ticket, because the funds could potentially be used to support the campaign of his opponent. More on that case is described in the viewpoint written by Adam Wolkoff for the Connecticut General Assembly in 2006, and are further studied by the Brennan Center for Justice.

Further studies show that despite the legal challenges, the publicly-funded campaigns have found success, including Democrat Janet Napolitano, who served as the governor of Arizona from 2003 to 2009. Supporters for publicly-funded elections at the national level include Massachusetts senator Elizabeth Warren, President Barack Obama, Arizona senator John McCain and Ralph Nader of Connecticut.

The following chapter examines states that run campaigns through public finance, the hurdles the legislation undergoes when passed, and if these measures have led to more or less successful than states that do not have the option to provide public funds to its candidates. The writers of these viewpoints, some of whom come from numerous policy-based organizations, describe a manner in which elections can be run that allows for expanded inclusion and transparency—one of the most important topics regarding the election in this current, heavily politicized political climate.

> "Following the case's dismissal
> in federal court and a series of
> state court decisions, the Arizona
> Supreme Court held that the
> surcharge was constitutional based
> on two principles articulated by the
> Supreme Court."

There Are Constitutional Issues to Public Financing of Campaigns

Adam Wolkoff

In the following viewpoint, Adam Wolkoff discusses the constitutional implications behind campaigns financed by public funds. Public financing laws, including those enacted in Arizona and Maine, have been challenged in the courts, but many of these laws have been upheld. The question behind the existence of these public campaign laws then turns to the extent in which the systems have made an impact in their respective states. Wolkoff includes summaries of two reports that have been published since 2005 and attempts to explain the impact of publicly-funded elections on the number and diversity of contributors and the amount of the contributions given to these publicly-funded campaigns. Wolkoff is an attorney and served as a law clerk to the Connecticut superior court.

"Public Financing Of Campaigns: Constitutional Issues And Impact," by Adam Wolkoff, Connecticut General Assembly, April 12, 2006.

As you read, consider the following questions:

1. In the case by Daggett challenging Maine's public finance laws, why did Daggett claim that the laws were unconstitutional?
2. What are the ways in which public campaign finance laws could potentially place undue burden on peoples' First Amendment Rights?
3. Why would people be against a surcharge on criminal and civil fines that would fund the public financing program, like the one challenged in Arizona?

While other states have limited public financing systems, only Arizona and Maine offer full state funding for gubernatorial, statewide office, and legislative candidates. Thus, this report focuses almost entirely on these two states.

Both Arizona and Maine faced legal challenges to their public financing laws, both of which became effective in 2000. Those who have brought the lawsuits, including candidates, lobbyists, and civil liberty advocates, have argued that public financing programs coerce involuntary participation, limit the ability of individuals and organizations to exercise free speech rights, and force taxpayers to subsidize candidates whose views they may oppose.

Yet state and federal courts have upheld the constitutionality of these laws, holding that public financing does not place an undue burden on the free speech or equal protection rights of (1) candidates who do not participate (i.e., nonparticipating candidates) or (2) their supporters. The Supreme Court declined to hear an appeal from at least one of these cases.

While courts have upheld public financing laws, the extent to which these systems have impacted elections is not yet entirely clear. The Campaign Finance Reform Working Group, which met last year to study changes to the election system, summarized a number of research reports on public financing, including a review of the General Accountability Office's (GAO) 2003 report on the

2000 and 2002 elections in Maine and Arizona (See, OLR Reports 2005-R-0191 and 2005-R-0620).

In that report, the GAO used five goals to determine the effectiveness of these programs. According to GAO, public financing systems are generally intended to (1) increase voter choice, (2) increase electoral competition, (3) reduce the influence of special interest groups, (4) curb increases in the cost of campaigns, and (5) increase voter participation. Based on its research, the GAO concluded that it was too soon to determine the extent to which the public financing programs have met their goals.

This report summarizes two reports we located since publishing our August 2005 report. One study analyzes the effect of public financing on the amount of time legislative candidates spent fundraising. The other report studies public financing's impact on (1) the number of contributors and their economic, geographic, and ethnic diversity, and (2) the size of campaign contributions.

Given the limited amount of new research available on the public financing of campaigns, it still appears to be too soon to make definitive conclusions about its impact.

Constitutionality

Maine

In 1996, Maine voters approved the Maine Clean Election Act by ballot initiative. The act established a voluntary system of full public financing for the primary and general election campaigns of gubernatorial and legislative candidates. To qualify for state grants, candidates must agree to forego private funding sources other than seed money and qualifying contributions, abide by spending limits, and comply with other program requirements. Under the act, participating candidates may receive supplemental funding, so-called "matching grants," when their nonparticipating opponents exceed the spending limit. Finally, the act reduces the amount of money that individuals and political action committees, known as PACs, may contribute to any candidate, regardless of whether he participates in the program.

Daggett v. Commission on Governmental Ethics and Election Practices (2000)

In 2000, the First Circuit Court of Appeals affirmed a district court decision upholding the constitutionality of Maine's public financing statute (*Daggett v. Commission on Governmental Ethics and Election Practices*, 205 F.3d 445 (1st Cir. 2000)).

In that case, ten plaintiffs challenged the act's constitutionality, including the National Right to Life PAC, the Maine Libertarian Party, and a group of legislative candidates represented by the American Civil Liberties Union. They argued that the public funding system unconstitutionally burdened the First Amendment rights of candidates by coercing them to become publicly funded. They also contested the constitutionality of providing matching funds and reducing contribution limits (*Daggett*, 205 F.3d at 452).

The *Daggett* court rejected these arguments. First, it upheld the constitutionality of contribution limits based on Maine's interest in preventing the appearance of corruption. It concluded that the limits were sufficient to allow a nonparticipating candidate to raise adequate funds to run a competitive campaign.

Second, the court held that the matching funds provision did not place an undue burden on the free speech of nonparticipating candidates because this program did not limit the quantity of speech a nonparticipant could engage in or the amount of money he could spend engaging in political speech.

Third, the court held that Maine's public financing system, as a whole, did not have the practical effect of forcing candidates to seek public funding. It found that the Maine act provided "a roughly proportionate mix of benefits and detriments to candidates seeking public funding, such that it does not burden the First Amendment rights of candidates or contributors" (Id. at 472).

The court pointed to one example of this "proportionate mix" in the limited scope of Maine's matching funds provision. Maine's act offers participating candidates matching funds totaling not more than two times the initial grant amount. The court noted that once a participant reached this limit, his nonparticipating opponent would still be able to outspend him. The court also noted that nonparticipating candidates could control how much and at what time their participating opponents received the matching funds. Such conditions demonstrated to the court that the act achieved a constitutionally-acceptable mix of benefits and detriments to participating and nonparticipating candidates.

Arizona

Arizona voters passed a ballot initiative in 1998, known as the Citizens Clean Election Act (CCEA), which created a voluntary public financing system for election campaigns. Under the act, Arizona provides participating candidates with an initial grant and matching funds if their nonparticipating opponents exceed the spending limit. Participating candidates may also receive compensation for money that third parties spend on advertisements advocating their defeat or their nonparticipating opponent's victory.

Since the act's passage, several cases have challenged the constitutionality of the system, according to the Brennan Center for Justice at the New York University School of Law. We summarize two leading opinions below.

Association of American Physicians and Surgeons v. Brewer (2005)

In 2005, a federal district court for Arizona upheld Arizona's public financing law (*Association of American Physicians and Surgeons v. Brewer*, 363 F.Supp.2d 1197 (D.Ariz. 2005)). In that case, the court expressly adopted the reasoning of the *Daggett* court, holding that Arizona's public financing program did not violate the First or Fourteenth Amendment rights of nonparticipating candidates.

Considering the plaintiffs' First Amendment challenges to the act's constitutionality, the court held that the system was not "impermissibly coercive," and that the state's interest in avoiding the appearance of corruption in elections was sufficiently compelling to warrant upholding the contribution limits required under the clean election law.

The plaintiffs also argued that the system violated the Fourteenth Amendment. They alleged that its system of classifying "independent expenditures" made by nonparticipating candidates and their supporters singled out certain forms of speech for disparate treatment, violating the fundamental right to political campaign speech. They also alleged that the system provided disparate treatment to nonparticipating candidates, violating their fundamental right to run as a privately supported candidate. The court rejected these arguments, holding that the government's interest in providing fair elections allowed the CCEA to pass constitutional scrutiny.

May v. McNally (2002)

In 2002, a state legislator challenged Arizona's public financing law on different First Amendment grounds than those in *Daggett*. Under the CCEA, Arizona imposes a 10% surcharge on criminal and civil fines to fund the public financing program. The legislator who brought the suit received a parking ticket but refused to pay the surcharge claiming it would violate his First Amendment right to free speech because the money could help pay for the campaign of a candidate with rival political views (*May v. McNally*, 203 Ariz. 245 (2002)).

Following the case's dismissal in federal court and a series of state court decisions, the Arizona Supreme Court held that the surcharge was constitutional based on two principles articulated by the Supreme Court.

First, the system was designed to further free speech, not impede it. The court cited the Supreme Court opinion in *Buckley v. Valeo*, 424 US 1 (1976), which held that the government could use public funds to establish a system of campaign financing. The *Buckley* court reasoned that public financing was designed "not to abridge, restrict, or censor speech, but rather [...] to facilitate and enlarge public discussion and participation in the electoral process, goals vital to a self-governing people" (*Buckley*, 424 US at 92-93).

Second, the court held that the surcharge did not infringe on the First Amendment rights of the legislator because the government's policy was "viewpoint neutral," or politically impartial. The court applied the Supreme Court's analysis in *Board of Regents v. Southworth*, 529 US 217 (2000), which held that a state university could allocate part of a mandatory student fee to student organizations conducting "ideologically expressive activities" as long as the university was viewpoint neutral in providing that support. Likewise, Arizona could dispense the proceeds of the surcharge to candidates as long as it did not discriminate on the basis of the candidate's political views.

The Supreme Court declined to hear an appeal of this case in 2003 (*May v. Brewer*, 538 US 923 (2003)).

Research on Public Financing

This report summarizes additional research we have found since the publication of OLR Report 2005-R-0191. As we noted in that report, studies on public financing's impact remain inconclusive because of the short length of time the laws in Arizona and Maine have been in effect (i.e., 2000).

"The Impact of Public Finance Laws on Fundraising in State Legislative Elections"

In their 2003 paper, "The Impact of Public Finance Laws on Fundraising in State Legislative Elections," University of Maryland political scientists Peter L. Francia and Paul S. Herrnson assessed the impact of public funding on the amount of time candidates devote to fundraising. They predicted that candidates who accepted full or partial public funding devoted less time to fundraising than candidates who received no subsidy.

The researchers mailed a nationwide survey in March 2001 to a random sample of candidates who ran for statewide, congressional, state legislative, local, and judicial offices between 1998 to 2000. They asked the candidates, "[A]pproximately what percentage of your personal campaign schedule was devoted to fundraising?" For the purposes of this study, Francia and Herrnson only analyzed data from state legislative candidates. Of the 6,644 questionnaires they sent to state legislative candidates, they received 2,317 responses from 50 states, a response rate of 35%.

The analysis controlled for variables including type of funding (full or partial public funding, or private funding), candidate characteristics (incumbent or other political experience), party identification, level of electoral competition, level of chamber competition, state campaign finance laws, term limits, and legislative professionalism (i.e., how desirable were the contested seats?).

The researchers generally concluded that candidates who accept public funding devote less time to fundraising, but that this benefit only appears in states with full, rather than partial, public funding. We summarize the specific findings below.

1. A "typical" legislative candidate who ran in a state that did not provide full or partial public funding spent 28% of his campaign schedule soliciting contributions.

2. In Maine and Arizona, the typical candidate who accepted public funding devoted on average only 11% of his campaign schedule to fundraising, while a nonparticipating candidate spent 27% of his time raising money.

3. In states with partial public funding, such as Hawaii, Minnesota, and Wisconsin, candidates who accepted funding actually devoted more time to fundraising than candidates who did not accept any funding (27% to 24%, respectively).

"Reclaiming Democracy in Arizona: How Clean Elections has Expanded the Universe of Campaign Contributors"
In its 2004 paper, "Reclaiming Democracy in Arizona: How Clean Elections has Expanded the Universe of Campaign Contributors," the Clean Elections Institute, an Arizona non-profit organization,

tracked the impact of public financing laws on Arizona's 1998 and 2002 gubernatorial campaigns, using data provided by the Institute on Money in State Politics. The 1998 campaign was the last gubernatorial race before the CCEA became effective.

The Clean Elections Institute determined that Arizona's public financing system, which requires candidates to collect $5 qualifying contributions to be eligible for funding, increased the number of contributors to gubernatorial campaigns. The total number of contributions to all candidates rose from 11,234 in 1998 to 38,579 in 2002. Meanwhile, the total number of candidates receiving "significant" numbers of contributors grew from two in 1998 to seven in 2002; of the seven, only one was a nonparticipant. The Institute also showed an increase in the geographic, economic, and ethnic diversity of the contributors.

The study found that the geographic diversity of contributors increased because participating candidates generally sought their required qualifying contributions from communities with which they had the closest ties. For example, one candidate garnered 54% of her contributions from her rural home county, which contained only 3% of the state's population.

Also, the study found that public financing increased the influence of lower income contributors, while decreasing the influence of higher income voters. It found that participating candidates secured up to 68% of their contributions from zip codes with per capita incomes below $40,000, while the nonparticipating candidates in 1998 and 2002 secured less than 30% of their contributions from these zip codes.

Finally, the Clean Elections Institute found greater ethnic diversity among contributors, especially Latinos, than before the CCEA was effective. It pointed to a Hispanic candidate who secured 59% of his contributors from zip codes with above average Latino populations.

Notably, the winner of the 2002 gubernatorial election, democrat Janet Napolitano, was a publicly funded candidate. According to the data in this report, her average contribution per donor was $12 and comparable to most of her participating opponents whose average contributions per donor ranged from $6 to $13. By contrast, the only nonparticipating candidate in the 2002 race had an average contribution of $293 per donor.

> *"Historically, many ethnic and racial minorities have been excluded from the political process, or have been led to feel that their presence was not welcome."*

Public Financing Fosters Electoral Diversity

Mimi Murray, Digby Marziani, Adam Skaggs

In the following viewpoint, Mimi Murray, Digby Marziani and Adam Skaggs argue that publicly-funded election laws can open the door for many other people, including and especially people in lower classes, to meaningfully participate in politics. The viewpoint includes multiple studies to back up the authors' claim, including a study from a professor at the University of Illinois that found that public funding programs in Maine and Arizona led to a decline in races with unopposed incumbents. The authors of the viewpoint also show how publicly financed campaigns lead to campaigns that focus more on the needs of the voter population as a whole, rather than the voices of few donors with deep pockets. Marziani and Skaggs are both former counsel for the Brennan Center for Justice's Democracy Program.

"More than Combating Corruption: The Other Benefits of Public Financing," by Mimi Murray Digby Marziani, Adam Skaggs, The Brennan Center for Justice, October 7, 2011. Reprinted by permission.

As you read, consider the following questions:

1. What are the major ways in which public financing fosters electoral diversity?
2. How do publicly financed elections lead to more competitive electoral races?
3. Why is it important that the Supreme Court determined the overall constitutionality of public financing?

Following the US Supreme Court's January 2010 decision in *Citizens United v. FEC*[2], a torrent of money has flowed into American elections. The 2010 elections that followed *Citizens United* were among the most expensive in our nation's history. Total spending was an estimated $3.6 billion[3]—an amount expected to rise dramatically in 2012. As the level of money involved in our elections steadily escalates, there is increasing concern about the ways that heightened campaign spending can purchase favorable policy outcomes.

Among the most vital tools to combat the corrupting influence of outsized campaign spending is public funding of elections. For more than three decades, public financing programs at the federal, state, and municipal levels have served, in the words of the US Supreme Court, "as a means of eliminating the improper influence of large private contributions . . . ."[4] Since the 1970s, federal courts have consistently relied upon the compelling governmental interest in curbing corruption in upholding public financing systems from constitutional challenge.[5]

But in June 2011, the US Supreme Court struck down a provision of Arizona's public financing system. In *Arizona Free Enterprise Club v. Bennett*, the court declared that Arizona's so-called trigger funds—additional public grants made available to a publicly funded candidate facing high opposition spending—burdened the First Amendment rights of those who opposed publicly funded candidates.

NON-PARTY CAMPAIGNS

Non-party campaigners are individuals or organisations that campaign in the run up to elections, but are not standing as political parties or candidates. In electoral law, we also call these individuals or organisations "third parties." There are rules on this campaigning.

There are two types of non-party campaigns.

These are:

- Local campaigns - non-party campaigns for or against one or more candidates in a particular constituency, ward or other electoral area
- General campaigns - non-party campaigns for or against a political party, or particular categories of candidates, including campaigns on policies or issues closely associated with a particular party or category of candidates (for example, candidates in a certain age group)

Campaigners spending more than a certain amount on general campaigning have to register with us.

There are limits on how much registered campaigners can spend. There are also controls on who can make donations and loans to them for the purpose of campaigning. Registered campaigners must record their campaign spending and donations they have received towards that spending. They must then send us this information in a spending return after the election.

We publish recognised third party spending returns online to ensure there is transparency about campaign spending at elections.

If you are thinking of campaigning in the run-up to an election but are not standing as a political party or candidate, please read our guidance for non-party campaigners.

"Non-party campaign spending and donations at elections," The Electoral Commission.

While the latest Supreme Court ruling will force changes to Arizona's public financing system (and other systems with similar trigger provisions), it contained a crucial silver lining for advocates of campaign finance reform: The Court affirmed the overall constitutionality of public financing. In unambiguous terms, the Court made clear that "governments may engage in public financing of election campaigns and . . . doing so can further significant governmental interests, such as the state interest in preventing corruption."[6]

As advocates and policymakers seek to respond to the growing levels of spending in elections by shoring up existing public financing systems and adopting new ones, it is crucial that they highlight the time-tested anti-corruption interests that public financing advances. They should also note several other benefits that flow from public financing.

Publicly funding elections promotes numerous benefits in addition to fighting corruption, all of which bolster the case for public finacing. By focusing exclusively on the significant anti-corruption benefits of public financing, advocates have sometimes overlooked these other ways that public funding programs enhance the legitimacy of government. Funding programs do not only reduce the opportunity for corruption and strengthen our perception of government; they also promote contested and competitive elections, foster diversity in the electoral process, and encourage voter-centered campaigns.

This memorandum presents the best available evidence of the lesser known benefits of public financing.

Public Financing Promotes More Contested and Competitive Elections

Few doubt that extraordinary Americans of ordinary means must have a meaningful ability to compete for elected office. Robust public funding programs open the door for qualified Americans who might not have personal wealth or high-powered connections by giving them the means to launch competitive campaigns. Several empirical studies confirm this conclusion.

- A 2010 study by a University of Illinois professor found that, in each election since their public funding programs were implemented, both Maine and Arizona have enjoyed a general decline in races with unopposed incumbents. In other words, with public financing, elected officials in those states are increasingly more likely to face a challenger when they run for re-election. [7]

- A 2008 study conducted by a Stanford Graduate School of Business professor similarly found that elections in Maine and Arizona between incumbents and publicly financed challengers are much more competitive than was true before public financing was adopted.[8] This finding confirms that public financing can provide newcomers with the ability to mount effective campaigns against incumbents.

- Further underlining that public funding increases the likelihood an incumbent will have a competitive race, a team at the University of Wisconsin-Madison found in a 2006 study looking at public financing in several states that public financing increases the pool of candidates willing and able to run for state legislative office. [9]

- A 2008 study by the director of the Yale Institution for Social and Policy Studies and a Fordham University professor found that radio advertisements which mentioned both major party candidates and encouraged listeners to vote resulted in incumbents' vote shares falling six to eight percentage points.[10] By allowing challengers to get their names out in front of voters, public financing causes elections to become more competitive than they otherwise would be.

- A 2010 study conducted by graduate students at New York University's Wagner School of Public Service compared electoral data in Maine and Arizona with states that have no public financing. The study found that public financing meaningfully increased the likelihood that incumbents would face real competition.[11] Overall, Maine's and Arizona's legislative races were more contested and more competitive than those in comparable states.[12]

- A study by a postdoctoral associate at Yale University concluded that public financing encourages experienced challengers within the incumbent party to run for open seats more often than they would without public financing.[13] Hence, public financing not only encourages more individuals to run, it also attracts high quality candidates.[14]

Consistent with these research findings, public financing is perceived as enhancing competition—both by candidates and the public. A Government Accountability Office study found that healthy percentages of candidates in states with public funding see it as a vehicle for spurring competition.[15] And a 2009 poll in North Carolina found that 85% of people surveyed agreed that "the high cost of campaigns means candidates must be good fundraisers to win—and the need to raise a lot of money keeps a lot of good people from serving in public office."[16] As a recent *New York Times* story on Connecticut's financing system put it, "For challengers, the appeal is obvious. Suddenly, they can have resources equal to an incumbent's without hitting up major donors."[17]

Other anecdotal evidence provides further support for the conclusion that public financing encourages competition. It is indisputable that the presidential public financing program has enabled several insurgent candidates from across the political spectrum to translate widespread popular support into viable campaigns.[18] The most notable example is Ronald Reagan, who depended heavily on public financing to challenge then-President Gerald Ford—backed by the Republican Party establishment—in the 1976 presidential primaries. Reagan had less than $44,000 in campaign money left at the end of that January, less than 10% of President Ford's war chest. Thanks to the presidential public financing system, however, Reagan was able to capitalize on his small-donor fundraising capacity to accrue substantial sums of public money—$1 million in January, $1.2 million more in February, and more still in March. These funds were pivotal in allowing Reagan to continue his almost-successful bid—ultimately, President Ford won by a hair.[19]

Public Financing Fosters Diversity in the Electoral Process

Facilitating new candidacies yields another significant benefit—diversity. As it invites more players into the electoral ring, public financing regularly enables members of traditionally underrepresented groups to run for political office.

Historically, many ethnic and racial minorities have been excluded from the political process, or have been led to feel that their presence was not welcome. For instance, after winning his seat on the Los Angeles City Council, Councilman Ed Reyes stated:

> My parents are from Mexico. I'm the first generation that has grown up here, I'm born here. I don't have the traditional ties to the power groups or the power structure. . . . Without public financing, I knew that I wouldn't have been able to throw a stone like in the David and Goliath story. . . . With public financing I knew I had a shot.[20]

The diversity-enhancing properties of public financing are widely documented:

- In a 2006 report from the Center for Governmental Studies, then-Project Director Steven Levin reported that while minorities represented only 16 percent of all candidates in general elections, they accounted for 30 percent of publicly financed candidates.[21] The rigorous study noted that while women accounted for only 31 percent of all candidates, they constituted 39 percent of participating candidates in publicly funded systems.[22] Finally, the study documented that in Arizona, the number of Native American and Latino candidates nearly tripled in just two election cycles after public financing was implemented.[23]
- In Congressional testimony presented in 2009, Jeffrey Garfield, the Executive Director of the Connecticut State Elections Enforcement Commission, stated that the number

of women running for office in Connecticut is at an all-time high—and many credit public financing with allowing them to run.[24]

- Similarly, in Maine, just a few years after the launch of that state's public financing program, women were reportedly taking advantage of public financing at a pace nearly double that of men.[25] The Center for Governmental Studies report cited above concluded that women are more likely to use Maine's public financing program than other candidates. [26] According to then-Maine Speaker of the House Hannah Pingree (D-ME), Maine's system has "increased the diversity of representatives in the legislature."[27]

- A Brennan Center report issued in 2010 documented a similar series of "firsts" resulting from New York City's small-donor matching funds system: the City's first African-American mayor, David Dinkins, participated in the program, as did the City Council's first Dominican-American, first Asian-American, and first Asian-American woman members.[28] Dan Cantor, Chair of the Working Families Party, points out that the "multiple match system has tremendously lowered the barrier to candidates who come from a background of service to communities and unions."[29] Although New York City, like many other state and local governments, does not maintain comprehensive demographic data, there is ample evidence that the use of the public financing system has been one of the principal reasons for the increasing diversity in the New York City Council.[30] In fact, the current City Council, as of the 2009 election, is "majority minority."

Publicly Financing Encourages Voter-Centered Campaigns

The majority of money brought in by major political candidates currently comes from a very small portion of the American population—America's "donor class."[31]

- According to data collected by the Center for Responsive Politics (and available on their website, OpenSecrets.org), only approximately 0.26% percent of the US population contributed $200 or more to federal political candidates, parties or PACs in the 2008 election—but these Americans contributed over 67% of all federal campaign dollars.[32]
- An analysis from the bipartisan Americans for Campaign Reform documented that residents of Manhattan's Upper East Side contributed $72 million in 2008, more than each of the bottom 39 states and approximately 50 times the national per capita rate.[33]
- According to a 2010 study by the Campaign Finance Institute, American Enterprise Institute and Brookings Institution, in 2008, US House incumbents received only 6% of their funds from donors who gave $200 or less. They received more than 13 times this amount from donors who gave $1,000 or more and from PACs.[34]
- An analysis of campaign contributions in the 2000 and 2002 elections found that almost 90% of contributions came from zip codes that are majority non-Hispanic white. In comparison, just 1.8% of campaign funds came from predominantly Latino zip codes, 2.8% from predominantly African American zip codes, and 0.6% from predominantly Asian Pacific American neighborhoods.[35]

Given the enormous financial demands of modern political campaigns, candidates too often focus on a tiny minority of known, wealthy donors—including non-constituents. The troubling result is that fundraising efforts do not reach most constituents, leaving them with less information about their potential representatives.

Public financing encourages voter-centered campaigning, drawing more voters into the political process. Public financing accomplishes this in various ways.

Under a full public financing system, participants must establish their eligibility by collecting a specified amount of small qualifying contributions from their constituents, necessarily contacting numerous constituents, and often bringing many new voters into the electoral process. After qualifying and receiving their full campaign fund grant, participating candidates focus nearly all of their campaign efforts on voter outreach.

Spurred by participating candidates' efforts to collect qualifying contributions, small donor participation in Arizona's gubernatorial races increased substantially after the implementation of that state's public financing program. A study of Arizona gubernatorial contributions found a three-fold increase from 11,234 in 1998 to 38,579 in 2002, with the majority of contributors earning $50,000 or less.[36] A similar three-fold increase occurred for other Arizona races.[37] Similarly, in Connecticut, most state legislative candidates who participated in the public financing program received money from a larger number of individual donors in 2008 than the predecessor candidate of the same party and district in 2006, the last year without the program.[38]

Cicero Booker, a Connecticut State Senate candidate from one of the state's poorer regions, recalled his experience collecting qualifying contributions. Many of the members of his district had never donated to a political campaign, but when they were told that small $5 contributions—normally inconsequential in enormously expensive fundraising campaigns—would help Booker qualify as a publicly financed candidate, they eagerly chipped in.[39] Similarly, of her experience running for Governor of Arizona as a fully-financed candidate, Janet Napolitano explained:

> [Public financing is] the difference between being able to go out and spend your time talking with voters, meeting with groups, . . . traveling to communities that have been underrepresented in the past, as opposed to being on the phone selling tickets to a $250 a plate fundraiser.[40]

Small donor matching funds systems provide even greater incentives for grassroots fundraising, particularly when small donations are supercharged with a high matching ratio. Candidates must seek out a broad base of small donors, and new voters are drawn into the electoral process as a result.

Take New York City's exemplary program. Serving millions of residents for more than twenty years, New York's program offers the highest matching ratio in the country—donations of $175 or less are matched with City dollars at a rate of six-to-one. In doing so, New York City has enhanced the importance of small donations, and has changed City campaigns for the better. A 2010 study from the Brennan Center reported that:

- The number of overall contributors has increased significantly—by 35%—since the enactment of the multiple match.[41]
- Participating candidates rely on more donors, and on more small donors, than do nonparticipants. In 2009, the typical participating City Council candidate enlisted the support of almost three times the number of small donors than did her nonparticipating counterpart.[42]
- In 2009, the average contribution to a participating City Council candidate was $199, substantially less than the $690 average contribution for non-participating candidates. Similarly, in 2005, the average contribution to participating City Council candidates was $321, significantly lower than the $804 average contribution for non-participants.[43]

Additional studies confirm the results documented by the Brennan Center. According to a report on New York City's program from the Campaign Finance Institute, in 2009 "1.75% of the city's voting age population contributed to candidates for city office." While this number may seem small, it is more than three times the 0.49% of the New York State voting population that contributed in state races. And, City contributions rose even in a year in which voter participation decreased.[44]

Including more voters in the electoral process naturally leads to a larger, more diverse pool of donors. For instance:

- According to the New York City Campaign Finance Board, the share of donor activity has risen in New York City's outer boroughs; in 2009, donor activity increased almost six-fold in Flushing, a heavily Asian-American neighborhood that is home to Queens' Chinatown.[45]

- Similarly, a scan of the occupations of 2009 donors to New York City elections reveals a surprisingly diverse group: among the traditional lawyers and businesspeople, contributors included a significant number of artists, administrative assistants, barbers and beauticians, cab and bus operators, carpenters, police officers, students, nurses, and clergy.[46]

Two midwestern states with partial public financing—Minnesota and Wisconsin—have also seen increased engagement with voters. One study by the Campaign Finance Institute found that in Minnesota, 57% of funds were received from donors who gave $250 or less in 2010; in Wisconsin, 36% of funds were in this amount.[47] Small donations in other Midwestern states that do not have public financing for legislative races—Illinois, Indiana, Michigan, and Ohio—fell between 3% and 12%.[48] The same study concluded that if small-donor matching programs were implemented in these states, a significant percentage of total candidate funds would come from small donors, with projections ranging from 61% to 72%.[49] Instead of courting an elite group of big donors, candidates instead would seek out small donations from the electorate at large.

As these examples make clear, public financing spurs greater involvement from members of the public.

One recent study found that small donors are more likely to volunteer for a political campaign.[50] Specifically, "surveys of candidates in six states show that the candidates see a strong connection between their small donors and the volunteer support that they get."[51]

Another study linked public financing with increased voter turnout in Arizona:

> Voter turnout increased by 8 percent, from 64 percent to 72 percent, between the 1996 presidential election (pre-Clean Elections) and the 2000 presidential election (the first under the

program). That number went up another five percentage points to 77 percent in the 2004 presidential. Similarly voter turnout increased by 10 percent, from 46 percent to 56 percent, between the 1998 midterm election . . . and the 2002 midterm elections.[52]

In short, publicly financed campaigns encourage a greater connection between would-be representatives and those they seek to serve, strengthening the electoral process and, ultimately, our democracy.

Laboratories of democracy in cities and states across the country have been experimenting with public funding programs for decades, and the myriad benefits of public financing are now evident. These programs not only reduce the opportunity for corruption and strengthen our perception of government; they also promote contested and competitive elections, foster diversity in the electoral process, and encourage voter-centered campaigns.

Notes

1. The authors give special thanks to David Early for his research assistance and meticulous citation checking, and to Michael Waldman and Wendy Weiser for their invaluable editorial assistance.

2. Citizens United v. FEC, 130 S. Ct. 876 (2010).

3. Ctr. for Responsive Politics, The Money Behind the Elections, OpenSecrets.org, http://www.opensecrets.org/bigpicture/index.php (last visited Aug. 24, 2011); see also FEC, Overview of Presidential Financial Activity 1996 – 2008, available at http://www.fec.gov/press/press2009/20090608Pres/1_OverviewPresFinActivit... (showing money received by presidential candidates from 1996 to 2008 increased by a factor of four).

4. Buckley v. Valeo, 424 U.S. 1, 96 (1976).

5. See, e.g., N.C. Right to Life Comm. Fund v. Leake, 524 F.3d 427 (4th Cir. 2008) (upholding North Carolina's judicial public funding system), cert. denied, Duke v. Leake, 129 S. Ct. 490 (2008); Daggett v. Comm'n on Governmental Ethics & Election Practices, 205 F.3d 445 (1st Cir. 2000) (upholding Maine's Clean Election Act); Rosenstiel v. Rodriguez, 101 F.3d 1544, 1552 (8th Cir. 1996) (upholding Minnesota's public funding system for elections); Vote Choice, Inc. v. DiStefano, 4 F.3d 26, 38 (1st Cir. 1993) (upholding Rhode Island's public funding system).

6. Id. at 2828 (quotations and citation omitted).

7. Michael G. Miller, Clean Elections vs. Political Speech 2 (2011), available at http://www.mainecleanelections.org/assets/files/Clean%20Elections%20v%20....

8. Neil Malhotra, The Impact of Public Financing on Electoral Competition: Evidence from Arizona and Maine, 8 St. Pols. & Pol'y Q. 263, 263 (2008).

9. Kenneth R. Mayer, Timothy Werner & Amanda Williams, Do Public Funding Program Enhance Electoral Competition?, in The Marketplace of Democracy: Electoral

Competition and American Politics 245 (Michael P. McDonald & John Samples eds., 2006).

10. Costas Panagopoulos, Leveling the Playing Field: Publicly Financed Campaigns and Electoral Competition, in Public Financing in American Elections 176, 182 (Costas Panagopoulos ed., 2011) (citing Costas Panagopoulos & Donald Green, Field Experiments Testing the Impact of Radio Advertisements on Electoral Competition, 52 Am. J. Pol. Sci. 156 (2008)).

11. This study was conducted at the Brennan Center's request. Annie Gleason, Daniel Ferris, Justin Eppley, Mucio Gudoy, Stephen Sumner & Xavier Smith, Elections and Public Financing 3 (2010) (unpublished report), available at http://www. followthemoney.org/press/Reports/Elections_and_Public_Financi....

12. See id. at 20.

13. Conor Dowling, Public Financing and Candidate Participation in Gubernatorial Elections, in Public Financing in American Elections, supra note 1010, at 184, 196.

14. Due to the impossibility of controlling all of the factors that determine the outcome in any particular election, it is extremely difficult to isolate the precise effect of public financing on electoral competition—or of any other electoral policy, for that matter. As a result, a few studies have announced inconclusive results when attempting to measure whether public funding spurs competition. For example, in 2010, the U.S. Government Accountability Office (GAO) completed an extensive study of the public financing programs in Maine and Arizona, including an inquiry into competitiveness. U.S. Gov't Accountability Office, Campaign Finance Reform: Experiences of Two States that Offered Full Public Funding for Political Candidates 4-5, 90-98 (2010), available at http://www.gao.gov/new.items/d10390.pdf. The GAO's findings on this topic were indisputably positive: They indicated, for example, that vote spreads were reduced in Maine and Arizona by a statistically significant amount, meaning those states had more close races and fewer landslide elections than similar states without public financing. Id. at 35-40. Ultimately, however, the GAO declined to definitely attribute this change to public financing, concluding that too many variables affect electoral competition.

15. Id. at 47-48.

16. Press Release, Democracy N.C., North Carolinians Across Political Spectrum Support Public Financing to Address Corruption (Dec. 9, 2009), available at http://www. democracy-nc.org/downloads/PPPPollPressRelease122009.pdf.

17. Peter Applebome, Connecticut Hopefuls Flock to Public Financing, N.Y. Times, Oct. 23, 2008, at A29, available at http://www.nytimes.com/2008/10/23/nyregion/connecticut/23towns.html.

18. Candidates benefitting from public financing include Ronald Reagan, Jimmy Carter, George H. W. Bush, Gary Hart, Jesse Jackson, Paul Tsongas, Pat Buchanan, John McCain, John Edwards, Wesley Clark, Richard Gephardt, and Joe Lieberman. Michael Malbin, Public Financing for Presidential Elections, in Public Financing in American Elections, supra note 10, at 36, 41-42. After President Barack Obama opted out of the presidential public financing system in 2008, there have been various calls to eliminate the program, and the House of Representatives voted in 2011 to abolish the program entirely. The proposal died in the Senate, and advocates have suggested that modifications to the presidential financing program—including replacing expenditure limits with lower contribution limits—would revive the program, spur greater candidate participation, and incentivize candidates to conduct outreach to small donors in lieu of large donors. See Anthony J. Corrado, Michael J. Malbin, Thomas E.

Mann & Norman J. Ornstein, Reform in an Age of Networked Campaigns: How to Foster Citizen Participation Through Small Donors and Volunteers 22 (2010), available at http://www.cfinst.org/books_reports/Reform-in-an-Age-of-Networked-Campai....

19. Michael Malbin, A Public Funding System in Jeopardy: Lessons from the Presidential Nomination Contest of 2004 in The Election After Reform: Money, Politics, and the Bipartisan Campaign Reform Act 219, 221 (Michael Malbin, ed. 2006), available at http://www.cfinst.org/pdf/books-reports/EAR/EAR_ch11.pdf; Brief for Amici Curiae Anthony Corrado, Thomas Mann and Norman Ornstein in Support of Respondents, Arizona Free Enterprise Club's Freedom Club PAC v. Bennett, 131 S. Ct. 2806 (2011) (Nos. 10-238 & 10-289), 2011 WL 661708.

20. Ctr. for Governmental Studies, Eleven Years of Reform: Many Successes — More to Be Done: Campaign Financing in the City of Los Angeles 23 (2001), available at http://www.cgs.org/images/publications/lacamp_fin.pdf.

21. Steven M. Levin, Ctr. for Governmental Studies, Keeping It Clean: Public Financing and American Elections 46-47, (2006), available at http://users.polisci.wisc.edu/kmayer/466/Keeping_It_Clean.pdf.

22. Id. at 47.

23. Id. at 7.

24. See A Look at H.R. 1826, and the Public Financing of Congressional Campaigns: Hearing on H.R. 1826 Before the H. Comm. on House Admin., 111th Cong. 206 (2009) [hereinafter A Look at H.R. 1826] (statement of Jeffrey Garfield, Exec. Dir., Conn. State Elections Enforcement Comm'n) (stating that in the 2008 Connecticut state elections more women had run for office than ever had previously).

25. Joshua Green, Clean Money in Maine, Am. Prospect (Nov. 30, 2002), http://prospect.org/cs/articles?article=clean_money_in_maine#.

26. Levin, supra note 211, at 39.

27. A Look at H.R. 1826, supra note 224, at 71 (statement of Speaker Hannah Pingree).

28. Angela Migally & Susan Liss, Brennan Ctr for Justice, Small Donor Matching Funds: The NYC Election Experience 21 (2010), available at http://www.brennancenter.org/page/-/Small%20Donor%20Matching%20Funds-The....

29. Id.

30. N.Y.C. Campaign Fin. Bd., New Yorkers Make Their Voices Heard: A Report on the 2009 Elections 142-43 (2010), available at http://www.nyccfb.info/PDF/per/2009_PER/2009PostElectionReport.pdf .

31. See Spencer Overton, The Donor Class: Campaign Finance, Democracy, and Participation, 153 U. Pa. L. Rev. 73, 76 (2004) ("While only 13.4% of American households earned at least $100,000 in 2000, these households gave 85.7% of contributions over $200 collected by presidential candidates.").

32. Ctr. for Responsive Politics, Donor Demographics 2010, OpenSecrets.org, http://www.opensecrets.org/bigpicture/donordemographics.php?cycle=2010 (last visited Aug. 25, 2011).

33. Ams. for Campaign Reform, Money in Politics: Who Gives (2010), available at http://www.acrreform.org/wp-content/uploads/2010/12/Fact-Sheet-Who-Gives....

34. See Corrado et al., supra note 18.

35. Pub. Campaign, Fannie Lou Hamer Project & William C. Velasquez Inst., Color of Money: Campaign Contributions, Race, Ethnicity, and Neighborhood 2 (2003), available at http://www.colorofmoney.org/report/com112103.pdf.

36. Ams. for Campaign Reform, Fair Elections: State Track Record of Success (2010), available at http://www.acrreform.org/wp-content/uploads/2010/12/Fair-Elections-State....

37. Levin, supra note 21, at 48.

38. Press Release, Campaign Fin. Inst., CFI's Review of Connecticut's Campaign Donors in 2006 and 2008 Finds Strengths in Citizen Election Program but Recommends Changes (Mar. 2, 2010), available at http://www.cfinst.org/Press/PReleases/10-03-02/Analysis_of_Connecticut_C....

39. See Conn. Common Cause, A New Kind of Politics: Citizens' Election Program Opening Politics to Connecticut's Citizens 3 (2008), available at http://www.commoncause.org/atf/cf/%7Bfb3c17e2-cdd1-4df6-92be-bd442989366....

40. Ctr. for Governmental Studies, Investing in Democracy: Creating Public Financing of Elections in Your Community 3 (2003), available at http://www.cgs.org/images/publications/investingindemocracy.pdf.

41. Migally & Liss, supra note 28, at 12.

42. Id. at 15 & n.113.

43. Id. at 15.

44. Michael J. Malbin & Peter W. Brusoe, Small Donors, Big Democracy: New York City's Matching Funds as a Model for the Nation and States 15 (2010) (unpublished report), available at http://www.cfinst.org/pdf/state/NYC-as-a-Model_Malbin-Brusoe_RIG_Dec2010....

45. N.Y.C. Campaign Fin. Bd., supra note 30, at 109-10.

46. Migally & Liss, supra note 28, at 13.

47. Michael J. Malbin, Peter W. Brusoe & Brendan Glavin, Campaign Fin. Inst., Public Financing of Elections After Citizens United and Arizona Free Enterprise 2 (2011), available at http://www.cfinst.org/pdf/state/CFI_Report_Small-Donors-in-Six-Midwester....

48. Id. Michigan has public financing for its gubernatorial elections. However, "[w]hile the program was effective for over 20 years, failure to amend it in recent years has rendered it obsolete" due to insufficient funding for candidates. Suzanne Novak & Lauren Jones, Brennan Ctr. for Justice, Campaign Finance in Michigan (2007), available at http://brennan.3cdn.net/b8d1f6b267641b2626_t0m6iiubp.pdf.

49. Malbin et al., supra note 4747, at 12-16.

50. Malbin & Brusoe, supra note 44, at 6-7.

51. Id.

52. Levin, supra note 21, at 49.

> *"Millard Fillmore and the Know-Nothings won 21 percent of the popular vote in 1856, but received only 2 percent of the electoral vote."*

Third Party Candidates Face a High Hurdle in the Electoral College

Walter Berns

In the following viewpoint, Walter Berns discusses the current two-party system in the United States and how the country has avoided electoral crisis in the years since its implementation. That said, Berns discusses how, despite the prevalence of the two-party campaign, candidates continue to run under the banner of a third party, be it Green or Libertarian or Independent or otherwise. Berns also details the constitutional process that would follow in an election in which no party achieves a majority and gives historical background on campaigns that have come close, including Millard Fillmore in 1856 and George Wallace in 1968. Berns is a resident scholar at the American Enterprise Institute and editor of After the People Vote: A Guide the Electoral College *(AEI Press, 1992), from which parts of this were adapted.*

"Third party candidates face a high hurdle in the electoral college," by Walter Berns, American Enterprise Institute, January 1, 1996. Reprinted by Permission.

As you read, consider the following questions:

1. Would an election in which neither major party candidate gains an Electoral College majority be a benefit or detriment to the country?
2. What are the long-term political and social implications of a third-party candidate getting enough Electoral College votes to prevent a major party candidate from getting a needed majority in a presidential election?
3. Though the two-party system has existed in the US for more than a century and a half, is it the best, most fair electoral system?

In the century and a half since the emergence of our current two-party system the United States has avoided any crisis in selecting a new president and vice-president–in part because the electoral college amplifies the margin of victory in the popular vote. This amplification gives us a clear winner even when the popular vote is close enough to be called a "photo-finish." John Kennedy, for example, won only one-third of a percent more popular votes than Richard Nixon in 1960, but collected 38 percent more electoral votes. Bill Clinton, who garnered just 43 percent of the popular vote in 1992's three-way race, captured nearly 70 percent of the electoral college.

It is always possible that a third–party candidate, by taking a state or two, may prevent either of the major party candidates from winning an electoral college majority, but this has not happened in the last 170 years. In such an event, the Constitution specifies that the election is thrown into the House of Representatives. It is quite likely, however, that in the weeks between the election and the gathering of the electoral college, the third–party candidate would entertain "bids" for his electors from one of the leaders–in return for policy or personnel concessions.

This was the express purpose in 1968 of George Wallace, who hoped to become kingmaker to either Richard Nixon or Hubert

Humphrey. Deadlocking the vote in the electoral college will always be a ticklish undertaking, however. A third party not only must capture some states, but must be careful elsewhere not to draw votes from only one of the two major candidates, thus giving the other a landslide.

Wallace's campaign turned out to be the most successful third–party bid in over 50 years. Yet while Nixon and Humphrey each received only 43 percent of the vote (Nixon just over and Humphrey just under), Nixon nonetheless picked up a decisive 56 percent of the electoral vote.

This occurred because the voting procedure of the electoral college deflates the strength of minor parties and inflates the margin of the winning party. By state law, all electoral votes (except Maine's and Nebraska's) are awarded on a winner-take-all basis to the candidate who captures the most votes within that state. To have any electoral effect, then, a party must win outright within states. Regional third–party challenges generally fare better under this system. Southern favorite Wallace actually captured 46 electoral votes. Yet the electoral college still deflated his challenge. Although he had received nearly 14 percent of the popular vote, he got only eight percent of the electoral vote. Some 4.1 million Wallace votes cast outside the states he carried were "wasted."

A third party with an even national appeal but lacking plurality support within any state will be stymied by the electoral college. Millard Fillmore and the Know-Nothings won 21 percent of the popular vote in 1856, but received only 2 percent of the electoral vote. Republican William Howard Taft was the choice of 23 percent of the voters in 1912, but of less than 2 percent of the electoral college. That same year, Theodore Roosevelt mounted the biggest third–party challenge of the twentieth century, taking 28 percent of the popular vote, yet he ended up with just 17 percent of the electoral vote. Most recently, we had Ross Perot's 1992 campaign, when he won nearly 20 percent of the popular vote but didn't earn a single electoral vote.

The fear of vote-wasting is the main psychological burden imposed by the electoral college's deflation of third–party efforts. As election day approaches, third–party candidates often see their support fade, because voters don't want to squander their ballot on someone who won't win. This happened to both Wallace and Perot.

Despite the failures of Theodore Roosevelt, George Wallace, Ross Perot, and others, it is always possible that a third–party candidate may prevent either of the major party candidates from winning the electoral college majority required by the Constitution. Recent changes in the law make this easier. Court decisions have made ballot access for third–party candidates simpler, and the Federal Election Campaign Act ensures public funding, in advance of an election, for any minor party that received at least 5 percent of the vote in the previous presidential race.

If ever someone mounts a third–party campaign that prevents an electoral college victory by one of the major parties, a little-known set of constitutional, statutory, and parliamentary rules governing the choice of a president and vice president would kick in: The newly sworn-in members of the House of Representatives, with one vote per state delegation, would choose the president from among the top three vote-getters in the electoral college. Support of at least 26 state delegations is required for a president to be selected. Simultaneously, the newly sworn-in members of the Senate would vote individually for vice president, choosing among the top two vote-getters in the electoral college, with 51 votes required for victory.

These mechanisms would produce a president and a vice president with unchallengeable constitutional claims to those offices. In a world where government succession is often bent to the dictates of force, the importance of this cannot be exaggerated.

"A second finding is, if these candidates are more visible, I'm more likely as a voter to see somebody on my stoop having a conversation with me, I might be more likely to vote."

Public Funding Drove Politicians to Spend More Time with Voters

Andrew Prokop

In the following viewpoint, Andrew Prokop interviews Michael G. Miller, a political science professor at Barnard College in New York, about the history of the Arizona Clean Elections Law, which was passed in 1998. One of the talking points in the months leading up to the law's passing was whether public financing of elections would lead to increased polarization. The Arizona Clean Election's Law was passed in response to a scandal in the 1990s regarding numerous Arizona legislators being either indicted or convicted on bribery charges involving the state's casinos. Prokop and Miller also discuss the quality of the campaigns run by candidates who may not have been able to run prior to the act that allowed elections in Arizona to be publicly funded. Prokop covers the US politics for Vox.

"After Arizona Passed Public Financing, Politicians Spent More Time with Voters," by Andrew Prokop and Ezra Klein, Vox Media, Inc., April 4, 2015. https://www.vox.com/2014/8/13/5996291/arizona-campaign-finance-system-explained. Reprinted by permission of Vox Media, Inc.

As you read, consider the following questions:

1. Why would a name like 'Clean Elections' encourage more people to vote in its favor, rather than against it?
2. What would be a conservative argument that Arizona's fees assessed on civil actions are a tax?
3. Why would it be difficult for a publicly-funded candidate to raise the minimum threshold to qualify for public funds?

In 1998, Arizona voters approved a historic overhaul of the state's campaign finance system. Under the Clean Elections Act, candidates for office are granted sizable public subsidies as long as they don't raise other money and abide by overall spending limits. Though reformers hoped this would help get money out of politics, some have argued that public financing could actually lead to increased polarization and dysfunction.

Michael G. Miller, a political science professor at Barnard College, and author of the book *Subsidizing Democracy*, surveyed over 1,000 candidates for office in states with public financing systems about their experience. I talked with him last year about what's happened in Arizona, and about his overall findings, below.

Andrew Prokop: How did the Arizona Clean Elections Law come about?

Michael G. Miller: There was a movement arising in the late 1990s that was largely in response to the AzScam scandal earlier in the decade, in which a number of Arizona legislators were either indicted or convicted for bribery charges involving casinos. There were gaming bills up and the legislators were effectively selling their votes. So, there was a huge scandal in the state, which led to this Clean Elections Act being proposed for the 1998 ballot. A lot of people saw it as a way to take money out of politics. The name of the bill, Clean Elections, was pretty ingenious, because who's going to vote against Clean Elections? A lot of voters may not fully have known what they were voting for, but they liked the sound of Clean Elections, particularly in the wake of AzScam.

Andrew Prokop: And what does the law actually entail?

Michael G. Miller: As originally passed, the bill would provide candidates for state office effectively with full public funding, so that they could have all the money that they needed from the public treasury—effectively eliminating private donations from the game. So, for example, if you were to run for Arizona House in the 2000 election, you first had to convince 210 people in your district to give you $5, exactly $5. That was the qualifying threshold. And it's actually quite hard to do, candidates will complain about the difficulties associated with raising what they call those "fives," they call them.

So, once you do that, you become eligible to receive public funding. In 2000, that amounted to a subsidy of $25,000, which was considered enough to run a viable campaign to run for Arizona statehouse. That subsidy has grown with time to reflect inflation. But for candidates running in these circumstances, when they accept these subsidies, they agree not to raise any more money from private sources, they agree not to spend more than the Clean Elections ceiling, and they agree not to bring any more of their money in. So once they receive these subsidies, effectively, it's game over for fundraising, and private money—be it from donors, or PACs, or whoever—is eliminated from the list of things they're allowed to solicit.

Andrew Prokop: Now, there was a US Supreme Court ruling in 2011 that struck down part of the law. What had to change?

Michael G. Miller: As originally designed, if a Clean Elections candidate were to run against a candidate who opted out of the program, and the the traditional candidate exceeded the Clean Elections subsidy in spending, the state of Arizona would issue the publicly funded candidate "matching fund" checks, locking the candidates in financial parity up to three times the original limit. So in 2000, you would've had to spend more than $75,000 as a nonparticipating candidate to outspend the Clean Elections candidate.

Overview of State-Level Public Financing

Public financing of campaigns remains the least-used method of regulating money in elections, partly due to the result of the US Supreme Court decision in *Buckley v. Valeo*. In that decision, the Court struck down a provision of the Federal Election Commission mandating public financing for presidential elections. States cannot require candidates to use public financing programs, and the financial advantages of private fundraising frequently prompt candidates to opt out of public financing programs, which often include expenditure limits for participants. Candidates who opt not to use public funds can solicit contributions from individuals, PACs, unions, parties, and corporations, without having to abide by state expenditure limits.

For states that elect to provide a public financing options, money is available for either individual candidates or political parties. This page provides information on both options, with examples of how the public financing option influenced a campaign.

Today, 14 states provide some form of public financing option for campaigns. Each of these plans require the candidate to accept public money for his or her campaign in exchange for a promise to limit both how much the candidate spends on the election and how much they receive in donations from any one group or individual.

In 2011, in *Arizona Free Enterprise Club Freedom Club PAC v. Bennett* and *McCormish v. Bennett*, the Supreme Court struck that down. The rationale for that decision was, if a traditional candidate runs against a Clean Elections candidate, the traditional candidate's incentive is to not spend because you are, in the words of candidates that I interviewed in my book, "feeding the alligator trying to eat me." So there was a First Amendment challenge brought, the argument was that, as applied, the matching funds provisions chilled the speech of nonparticipating candidates. And the Supreme Court agreed with that.

The two main types of programs states offer for public financing of elections are the clean elections programs offered in states such as Maine and Arizona, and programs that provide a candidate with matching funds for each qualifying contribution they receive.

In the clean elections programs offered only in Arizona, Connecticut, Maine, candidates are encouraged to collect small contributions (no more than $5) from a number of individuals (depending on the position sought) to demonstrate that he or she has enough public support to warrant public funding of his or her campaign. In return, the commission established for the program gives the candidate a sum of money equal to the expenditure limit set for the election. New Mexico offers a similar program, but only for judicial candidates.

As an example of a clean elections program, a candidate for state office in Arizona must raise $5 contributions from at least 200 people in order to qualify for the program. In return, the state provides the candidate with public money in an amount equal to the expenditure limit. In the 2014 election, the expenditure limit for gubernatorial candidates was $1,130,424, and the limit for legislative positions was $22,880.

"Overview of State Laws on Public Financing," National Conference of State Legislatures.

Andrew Prokop: You wrote a book, *Subsidizing Democracy*, that analyzed how public financing has worked in Arizona and other states. What did you find?

Michael G. Miller: The book examined how public funding changes the behavior and emotions and strategy of candidates that are in these elections. Connecticut and Maine have very similar programs, so I did survey work and interviews with candidates Arizona, but also in those other two states. I looked at candidates in Hawaii, Wisconsin, and Minnesota, which at the time had different kinds of smaller, partial public funding. I really worked with these folks in-depth to determine how they were using their time, their attributes, their qualifications, and their strategic consideration.

One of my findings was that candidates who accept these subsidies are much more likely to interact with voters on a weekly basis, to the tune of about 5 hours. The reason for that is they don't have to raise money. So the time they would've spent raising money is directly reinvested into voter engagement. So they're doing a lot more knocking on doors, they're doing a lot more meetings with interest groups, interviews with media, speeches, things like that. So they're more visible. And over the course of a 30 week campaign, 5 hours a week really adds up. You're talking about hundreds or thousands of interactions with voters that would not have occurred in the absence of public funding. That's one argument in the book.

A second finding is, if these candidates are more visible, I'm more likely as a voter to see somebody on my stoop having a conversation with me, I might be more likely to vote. And that's what I find. I find about a reduction of 20 percent in rolloff. So that is, people who show up to vote for, say, president in 2008, and then stop voting when they get to the statehouse races—that more people stick around and vote in those downballot elections. Presumably that's because they have seen these candidates, they've had these interactions with them. So you get more participation among the electorate.

Another of my findings is that it's easier for so-called average people who may not have run for office to hit the ground with a really impactful, what political scientists would call "high-quality," campaign. And the reason is because they have money. Say you're a teacher or a plumber, or somebody else who's never run for office before. It's hard to build those connections and relationships [that are necessary for high-dollar fundraising]. These subsidies —the term I use in the book is that they "manufacture" quality challengers. And political scientists found that incumbents still usually win, but they win by smaller amounts. So you get elections that are a little more competitive, and I think one of the reasons for that is you're allowing average folks to command the resources commensurate with a strong campaign.

Finally, there's a chapter in the book about the objections that conservative candidates have to [using public funds for their campaigns]. And you really do see disproportionate participation between Democrats and Republicans, largely based on comfort level with the utilization of public money for this purpose.

Andrew Prokop: What are the differences between the various public financing programs that exist in the US?

Michael G. Miller: Arizona, Maine, and Connecticut all fund state candidates pretty broadly. The differences between their systems are pretty esoteric. There used to be differences in matching funds allocations but those are gone now.

One major difference of Arizona's is the way it's funded. Arizona's unique in that it's not supposed to appropriate money from its general fund, so it uses fees assessed on speeding tickets and other civil actions. So in theory, it's not tax dollars. Although conservatives will argue that anytime a dollar leaves your pocket and goes to government it's a tax—that it's a matter of semantics. But it's unique in that way. My advice would be not to get caught speeding in Arizona, because there is that charge.

Andrew Prokop: What's your impression about how this changed politics in Arizona, broadly? How did it change governance and the functioning of the legislature? Did things become more ideological?

Michael G. Miller: There are several papers right now that trying to suss that question out. One argument is that if you don't have to raise money in the private marketplace of campaign finance, you can be a really extreme candidate. You hear these stories in Arizona of really far-right candidates going to one of those big churches and putting their qualifications packet in the offering plate and passing it around and getting their "fives" in twenty minutes. Then they can go—they don't have to worry about how they'll get donations despite extreme views.

So the argument is that these public funding candidates are more ideologically extreme than candidates who have to raise money from private donors. But a paper I have with Seth Masket [from the University of Denver] finds effectively no difference in the ideological position between the two groups of candidates.

We are at odds with another paper by Andrew Hall, a graduate student at Harvard, who is reporting more extreme candidates. [NOTE: Hall's paper also argues that states that adopted public funding subsequently became more polarized than states that did not.] It's an unresolved question, but I believe my paper more than other papers out there right now.

Andrew Prokop: Arizona's legislature last made national news for adopting a tough anti-illegal immigration law in 2010. Would you say that the public financing system made that more likely to pass? Support for loosening immigration laws is more widespread among business interests, and under public financing, the support of business may be less important to candidates.

Michael G. Miller: I think that theory's plausible, but I just don't see it in the data, and I always follow the data. So what I have found in my work is that there's no relationship between accepting public funding and taking more extreme positions. As I said, the narrative has always seemed plausible to me, and I actually was a little surprised when we found no relationship. But I just don't see it in the data. You've got to bear in mind, Arizona's still a really unique place politically, they have a strong strain of libertarianism running through the right side of their politics. It's a very perceptible tinge of American conservatism. Barry Goldwater's alive and well in his home state.

I think there's a temptation to look for these explanations when we see extreme politics happening in a place, but I think it really is as simple as—if you look at the dynamics of the state, it is kinda a microcosm of America in many ways and you see same kinds of things happening there as you do in the United States Congress. And there's no public funding in the United States Congress. So I think, we tend to go on these hunts for explanations, when it just ends up being the way things are due to political history, culture, or larger dynamics.

> *"Only public financing can ensure that tax dollars are spent in the interests of all the people, not wasted in order to pay back campaign contributors."*

Public Financing Is in the Interest of All People

Joan Mandle

In the following viewpoint, Joan Mandle discusses the scope of public concern regarding public financing in elections. Mandle points out the low annual costs for nationally public-financed elections, and also the numerous myths surrounding public perception of campaign finance reform. Mandle lists 10 states that have laws in place for publicly-financed elections—in which polling reveals that there is widespread concern regarding the electoral process, and that money from major campaign contributors, also known as "big money" is corrupting the American political system. The viewpoint also details the number of shortcomings involved with publicly-funded elections, in that public financing is voluntary, meaning that all the candidates do not have to participate, which could put the candidates that do at a disadvantage. Mandle is executive director at Democracy Matters.

As you read, consider the following questions:

1. Per the viewpoint, would publicly-funded elections raise taxes? Why or why not?
2. Is $10 a year per person a feasible amount of money to pay for national, publicly-funded elections?
3. Is so-called "big money" corrupting politics in the US? Why or why not?

Not With My Taxes, You Don't.

Many people are concerned that public financing will raise taxes. But taxpayers actually save money if politicians are not funded by special interests in return for tax breaks, special favors, and government bailouts. Only public financing can ensure that tax dollars are spent in the interests of all the people, not wasted in order to pay back campaign contributors.

It is estimated that public financing would cost less than $10 a year for each taxpayer in the United States. (In states and cities with public financing systems it costs even less!) It would mean that politicians would be working for all the people, not just those who fund their campaigns. Ten dollars a year seems little to pay in order to ensure a true democracy, where everyone has an equal say in the votes cast by elected officials.

I Don't Want To Support Corrupt Politicians Or David Duke.

Public financing will support all eligible and serious candidates. Criteria are set to make sure that candidates with no real support cannot qualify for public funds. However, all serious candidates will have an equal chance to qualify for public financing, regardless of their views. This is democracy at work—everyone has an equal chance to air their opinions, as well as to object to the views of others.

Voters in this system will—for the first time—have a real choice among a wide diversity of candidates. If a politician is corrupt or has loathsome views, challengers supported by public financing will be able to communicate this information to the voters. In the present system anyone with offensive views can run if she/he has the money. Public financing gives voters more choice, more information, and more diversity of candidates. Together these help create a strong democracy.

No One Cares About Campaign Finance Reform.

Polling indicates that there is widespread concern about our electoral process. Polls have shown that a large majority believes that big money is corrupting our political system and favors getting private money out of politics. They understand the extent to which big private money is silencing the voices of ordinary citizens.

Citizens in Maine, Arizona, North Carolina, Wisconsin, Connecticut, Vermont, New Mexico, New York City, Los Angeles, and Albuquerque, NM care so much about full public financing that they have fought for and won public financing laws in their cities and states.

I Won't Support Wasteful Spending.

The best way to rid our government of wasteful spending is to eliminate the dependence of politicians on wealthy donors and special interests who want pay-backs for their funding of campaigns. This is the heart of the corruption that regularly returns incumbents to office with their huge fundraising advantage over challengers. Typically 95%–99% of Congressional incumbents are re-elected and returned to office, even though Congress's public approval rating is below 20%. Typically the average Congressional incumbent candidate will spend 4 or 5 times more money than their challengers. With public financing, the playing field is more even among candidates, and when publicly financed candidates are elected, our tax dollars go where they belong—to public needs rather to pay back wealthy special interests. That's the real source of waste.

The Rich Will Always Prevail By Outspending Everyone.

The system of public financing is voluntary. A candidate who refuses to take public funds and abide by spending limits can raise and spend as much as he or she wants to. However, public financing offers other candidates the chance to get their message out to the public to win support. After a certain point, additional spending does not mean as much. In addition, publicly funded candidates can and do point out that unlike those dependent on private funding, if elected they will be beholden to all the people and not just to big campaign funders. Maine and Arizona have shown that publicly financed candidates can be elected even if outspent. In those states between 70 and 85% of elected officials have run with public financing.

This Has Never Worked Before.

Public financing systems have been working well for decades in a number of states and cities. This experience proves that the system deepens democracy. Presidential public financing worked well for over 30 years. Furthermore, in almost all democratic countries other than the United States, including Canada, Australia, France, and Germany, extensive systems of public financing are in place. Public financing has created more competitive elections, more diverse candidates, less power to big funders, and real choice for voters.

I Am Too Busy Working To Protect The Environment, For Women's And Civil Rights, For Health Care, Or Global Justice.

Public financing of elections affects ALL the issues mentioned above and hundreds of others as well. Public financing is the reform that allows all other reforms to be accomplished. It ensures that elected officials are responsive to the majority of the electorate rather than to the tiny elite that funds their campaigns. By providing public funding for campaigns of those who care about the environment, about America's role in the world, about education spending, heath care, civil rights and so much more, we can elect legislatures willing to vote for the reforms that most Americans support.

It's Unconstitutional.

The courts have consistently upheld the public financing of election campaigns as constitutional. They have however—including the Supreme Court in its *Buckley v. Valeo* decision—consistently expressed concern about reforms that would limit the amount of contributions to or spending in campaigns. They have done so primarily because of free speech considerations—the argument that to constrain contributions or spending would limit the political discourse.

But public financing does just the opposite. It allows for more political speech by a larger and more diverse group of candidates. In that sense, it enhances free speech by providing more individuals an opportunity to get their political message out to the public and perhaps be elected to office as a result. With the fair funding that public financing represents, not only those who can call on wealthy special interests to fund their campaigns can speak, but anyone who is a serious candidate. Rather than limiting it, public financing broadens the political dialogue and in this way enhances democracy. Though the conservative members of the Supreme Court are attacking campaign finance reform, they have not been able to destroy public campaign financing because they believe it is consistent with the Constitution.

Full Disclosure And Ethics Reforms Are Enough.

Full disclosure of the names and occupations of major campaign contributors of course is essential to the democratic process. The public has the right to know to whom and to what interests its elected officials are beholden. Electronic filing — using the internet to enhance disclosure—is an important step in giving the public access to this information. Strong ethics laws that can respond to the many money scandals are critical as well. And we need disclosure of "dark money" and independent *Super PAC* spending.

However, these reforms are not enough. Disclosure is the law in most elections and yet this has done nothing to stop the flood of money to candidates. It is not realistic to expect that in a country where less than half the people even vote, most citizens will make the effort and devote the time needed to analyze political contributions.

Only the public financing of elections can ensure a more level playing field so that donations to candidates are not the prime determinant of who runs, who is elected, and what social policies they support. Only public financing can create a democracy in which any citizen can run for office, where merit rather than money decides who wins, and where all citizens can have an equal influence in elections.

The Presidential Public Financing System Is Broken.

The Presidential public financing system was created in 1976 as part of Federal Election Campaign Act. Congress thought that the Presidential race was so important that candidates should not have to depend on wealth or the ability to raise large sums of money. In addition there was concern (even then!) that constant increases in campaign spending were spiraling out of control. The Congress gave Presidential candidates the option to limit their spending and in turn receive public financing – partial matching funds in the primary and full funding in the general election. Every candidate for President participated in this public financing system until 2000, when George Bush refused public matching funds in the primary in favor raising private funds for his campaign. The Congress neglected to raise the amount of public funds available to candidates and so by 2008 most major candidates were not participating in the public system because it underfunded them and they could raise much more by taking private money.

However, the breakdown of the Presidential public financing system does not mean that public financing can't work. What it shows is that we need a better system of public financing—like the one that is working so well in states and cities. And the Presidential public financing system needs to be fixed by providing generous public funding to candidates.

Privately Financed Elections Don't Cost Taxpayers Anything.

The actual cost of privately funded elections may not come from tax money but the consequences of this system are costing taxpayers billions of dollars. These consequences include myriad tax breaks, subsidies, regulatory exemptions, bail-outs and other favors that elected officials regularly perform for their financial backers. As Public Campaign reported: "Every year, the average American taxpayer shells out more than $1000 in federal income taxes so the government can keep some very important taxpayers on welfare. Those taxpayers are better known as corporations, and according to a trenchant series in Time magazine by investigative reporters Donald Barlett and James Steele, a privileged group of well-connected and savvy businesses milk $125 billion a year out of the US Treasury in grants, subsidies, low-interest loans, tax credits, exemptions, deductions and deferrals."

There are serious costs also in costly government policies that the majority of the American people disagree with, like the trillions of dollars in military spending in the Middle East, or the investment in the development of fossil fuels rather than renewable energy.

Special Interests Balance Each Other Out.

There is a vast array of "special interests" who try to influence legislation. But some are more powerful than others. Here are just a few examples of total contributions to federal campaigns and parties from 1990 to 2014 (Center for Responsive Politics https://www.opensecrets.org/industries/):

- Energy and Natural Resource Industries $365 Million
- Pro-Environment Contributions $130 Million
- Finance, Real Estate & Insurance $3.8 Billion
- Misc. Business $2.3 Billion
- Agribusiness $698 Million
- Labor $1.2 Billion
- Liberal Ideology $144.3 Million
- Gun Rights $34.1Million
- Gun Control $2.0 Million

Money Only Buys Access—Not Votes.

"Senators and representatives, faced constantly with the need to raise ever more money to fuel their campaigns, can scarcely avoid weighing every decision against the question 'How will this affect my fundraising prospects?' rather than 'How will this affect the national interest?'" —former US Senator Barry Goldwater (R—Arizona)

"What goes on every day in Sacramento is that the same lobbyist comes in, and on Monday he talks to you about how he's arranging for a campaign contribution from a client. And on Tuesday he comes back and asks you to vote on a piece of legislation for that same client." —former State Senator Alan Robbins (D—California)

"The payoff may be as obvious and overt as a floor vote in favor of a contributors' desired tax loophole or appropriation. Or it may be subtle…a floor speech not delivered…a bill pigeon-holed in subcommittee…an amendment not offered, or a private conversation with four or five key colleagues in the privacy of the cloakroom." —former US Senator William Proxmire (D—Wisconsin)

Contributing Money Is An Important Way To Participate.

Making sure that citizens participate in a democracy is important, but it is just as important to make sure that everyone has an equal opportunity to participate. That's why each citizen has one and only one vote. But because wealth is so unequally distributed in the United States, not everyone has an equal opportunity to participate by contributing funds to candidates. In fact, in our privately funded campaign system, contributing to campaigns violates the ideal of equality in a democracy, for only those with money can spend the maximum and have the maximum influence. In most elections less than 1% of citizens contribute significantly (more than $200) to political candidates. That means those people and interests use their wealth to have greater influence—to participate more, while others are silenced by their inability to contribute large amount.

Although a few candidates, have successfully used the internet to attract many small donors, the fact remains that the majority of their funding came from traditional big donors, based in the corporate sector. And in the Congress, the role of small donors has actually DECLINED over time while the power of mega-donors has increased. Fair Elections public financing is a real small donor system! It matches small donations with public funds (often with six public dollars for every dollar raised—as in New York City.) Candidates elected by public financing systems do not have to be rich and are not dependent on rich donors. Once elected they are accountable to their donors—the public not to the wealthy 1%!

Congress Will Never Pass A Bill For Public Financing.

Never is a very long time, and things change rapidly in politics! Every year since 2010 the Fair Elections Now Act and Government by the People Act have been introduced as Congressional bills. Both include public financing and other reforms. By 2015, there were over 130 co-sponsors in the House including the Speaker of the House who endorsed this legislation, and many in the Senate as well. Senator Durbin, sponsor of Fair Elections, has stated that the banks own Congress and said he will continue to fight for this legislation because democracy can't afford to be destroyed by the flood of money to Congressional campaigns. What Congress needs is a strong grassroots social movement (like the kind Democracy Matters and our allies are building) to force it to do what is right and pass this legislation (just as the civil rights movement forced Congress to pass civil rights legislation, and the environmental movement of the '70s forced passage of the Clean Air and Clean Water Acts.)

I've Given Up On Reform Since Citizens United & Mccutcheon

It's certainly true that the 2010 Supreme Court decision unleashing unlimited corporate spending on political speech through *Super PACs*, and its McCutcheon decision two years later have made the problem of corporate big money influence in politics much worse.

BUT that is exactly why we are building a national grassroots movement for reform. Both the efforts to reverse Citizens United and the fight to create a public financing option for candidates are even more important now. That is the only way candidates and our political system can be independent of the total domination by corporate money. Over 80% of Americans disagreed with Citizens United and McCutcheon.

People from all walks of life are outraged by increasing flood of corporate money in each election cycle. They want a government of, by, and for the people—not the corporations. We need to join together to save our democracy. If not you... then who? If not now... then when? Join us!!

Periodical and Internet Sources Bibliography

The following articles have been selected to supplement the diverse views presented in this chapter.

Bruce Ackerman & Ian Ayres. "Voting with Dollars: A New Paradigm for Campaign Finance," New Haven, Yale University Press, 2002.

Peter Applebome, "Connecticut Hopefuls Flock to Public Financing, N.Y. Times, Oct. 23, 2008," at A29, available at http://www.nytimes.com/2008/10/23/nyregion/connecticut/23towns.html.

"Designing Public Financing Systems to Advance Equity and Independent Political Power," Demos, February 5, 2016. http://www.demos.org/publication/designing-public-financing-systems-advance-equity-and-independent-political-power

International Foundation for Electoral Systems (IFES), "Enforcing political finance laws. Training Handbook. Training in detections and enforcement (TIDE)", Washington, June 2005.

Adam Lioz, "Stacked Deck: How the Racial Bias in Our Big Money Political System Undermines our Democracy and Our Economy", Demos, (2014). http://www.demos.org/publication/stacked-deck-how-racial-bias-our-big-money-political-system-undermines-our-democracy-a-0.

J. Mijin Cha & Miles Rapoport, "Fresh Start: The Impact of Public Campaign Financing in Connecticut", Demos, (2013). http://www.demos.org/publication/fresh-start-impact-public-campaign-financing-connecticut

Costas Panagopoulos, "Leveling the Playing Field: Publicly Financed Campaigns and Electoral Competition", in Public Financing in American Elections 176, 182 (Costas Panagopoulos ed., 2011)

Nate Silver, "New Rove Group Could Backfire on G.O.P.", The New York Times, February 11, 2013 http://fivethirtyeight.blogs.nytimes.com/2013/02/11/new-rove-group-could-backfire-on-g-o-p

World Economic Forum and Transparency International, "Partnering Against Corruption Initiative", 2005. http://www.weforum.org/issues/partnering-against-corruption-initiative

Why Is Private Campaign Financing the Most Popular Way to Raise Funds?

Chapter Preface

For better or for worse, money and elections are tied together so tight that it seems that it's impossible to unravel them. Part of this unhealthy relationship stems from the fact that, no matter what, it takes money to run a campaign in which tens of millions of eligible citizens United States get out and vote. From the earliest days of American government, money has played a factor in one way or another.

In the viewpoints in this chapter, many contributors point out that there is a significant consensus in the United States that, though campaign finance has been reformed in the years since the 1971 establishment of the Federal Election Campaign Act and the 1974 amendments that established the Federal Election Commission, the system is still in dire need of further reform.

One of the many reforms that have been established so far in campaign finance is the limits of how much an individual can donate to a candidate that is campaigning at the federal level. These contribution limits open a door that allows more people to feel as though their political contribution holds weight, that it matters to their preferred candidate's success, but contribution limits are easily subverted, especially by corporations and donors whose pockets are deep.

Additionally, the following chapter focuses on the most common way candidates raise funds: through private financing. These diverse viewpoints explore just how much influence the richest percentages of people in the United States have over elections and the establishment of public policy and attempt to grapple with what may very well be a broken campaign finance system.

*"If a candidate opts into this program,
he or she makes certain promises to
not raise private capital, and can
only spend on their campaign an
amount established by the state."*

State Campaign Finance Laws Have a History

National Conference of State Legislatures

In the following viewpoint, writers from the National Conference of State Legislatures (NCSL) detail an overview on the history of campaign finance laws in the United States. The NCSL states that there is no way to answer the question of how much a role money should play in politics and goes on to describe three ways states should regulate campaign finance: disclosure, contribution limits, and the public financing of elections. Additionally, the NCLS points out that, because the federal government leaves elections largely up to state governments, there is no standard form of election regulation. The National Conference of State Legislatures is a bipartisan organization that serves US state legislatures.

"State Campaign Finance Laws: An Overview," National Conference of State Legislatures. Reprinted by permission.

As you read, consider the following questions:

1. Of the three ways to regulate the role of money in politics listed by the NCSL, which is the best option and why?
2. Should there be federal regulation of state-run elections? Why or why not?
3. Would a consistent regulation of campaign finance in state elections benefit elections that take place at the federal level? Why or why not?

In 1757, George Washington spent about $195 for food and drinks to help win election to the Virginia House of Burgesses. This practice of using money or gifts to influence the outcome of an election would soon be abolished by the Virginia legislature, but it remains an important issue for today's legislators. All 50 states regulate the way money is spent in politics and elections, publishing entire code sections dedicated to providing accountability and transparency in this area. The cost of elections and campaigns continues to rise, and candidates are forced to rely on contributions from the private sector to fund the ever-increasing costs. Seen by many as a natural extension of an individual's freedom of speech, using money to influence elections troubles those who believe money can have a corruptive influence on candidates. State legislators wishing to change their state's campaign finance laws must be sensitive to these separate views, while adhering to the principles set forth by Supreme Court decisions that further alter the role of money in politics.

This page provides an overview of commonly used methods to regulate campaign finance, as well as influential court decisions that helped shape this regulation. To see a list of campaign finance bills that legislators have introduced in 2015, see NCSL's 2015 Campaign Finance Legislation Database (http://www.ncsl.org/research/elections-and-campaigns/campaign-finance-database-2015-onward.aspx).

How Do States Regulate Campaign Finance?

As there is no right answer to the question of how large a role money should play in politics, there are many methods used to regulate campaign finance. The three discussed below are the most common. These methods include: 1) the imposition of disclosure and reporting requirements, 2) setting contribution limits to candidate's campaigns, and 3) providing a method for public financing of elections. Because the federal government leaves elections largely up to the states, the methods used by each state varies dramatically. To learn more about types of restrictions imposed by states, follow the links below each subheading.

Disclosure

The most common means of regulating political spending is through various disclosure and reporting requirements. All 50 states mandate that candidates for elective office report the contributions they receive and the expenditures they make while pursuing public office. This area of campaign finance is constantly evolving, so please see NCSL's 2015 Campaign Finance Legislation Database for examples of laws, introduced this year, that deal with disclosure requirements.

Contribution Limits

The second most common means of regulating money in elections is through the imposition of limits on the amount of money any group or individual can contribute to a campaign. This area has grabbed the most attention, with recent Supreme Court cases bringing contribution limits to the forefront of the campaign finance debate.

Public Financing of Elections

A third method states use to regulate spending in elections is by providing a means by which candidates can accept public funds to conduct their campaign. This approach mirrors the federal public financing option, which was instituted by the FEC in 1974. If a candidate opts into this program, he or she makes certain promises to not raise private capital, and can only spend on their campaign an amount established by the state.

Campaign Finance and the Supreme Court

Though legislators have no say in how the Supreme Court interprets campaign finance laws, the Court's decisions force lawmakers to adapt to the changing legal landscape. This page (http://www.ncsl. org/research/elections-and-campaigns/campaign-finance-and-the-supreme-court.aspx) outlines some of the most important Supreme Court decisions on campaign finance, with emphasis on how states have adapt to the rulings of the nation's highest court. Rulings from other federal and state courts also dramatically impact campaign finance, but their impacts are geographically limited and not included in this page.

> "Under FECA, it would be next to impossible for a candidate to launch such a late starting campaign, unless ... the candidate was a multimillionaire capable of funding his or her own campaign."

Limits on Campaign Contributions Stifle Citizens' Power

Bradley A. Smith

In the following excerpted classic viewpoint, Bradley A. Smith discusses the impacts of soft money in the United States' presidential campaigns. While soft money donations were unlawful for a brief period in the 1970s, the ban was never intended to be implemented by that Congress, and per the viewpoint, the likelihood of soft money being banned from presidential elections is unlikely. Smith also discusses how the limits on campaign contributions, specifically how much an individual can donate to one candidate, stifles political speech and can infringe on a candidate's First Amendment rights. The viewpoint also details overall impact of the Federal Election Campaign Act of 1974. Smith served as Commissioner, Vice Chairman and Chairman of the Federal Election Commission between 2000 and 2005.

"Campaign Finance Reform: Soft Money and the Presidential Campaign System," by Bradley A. Smith, Cato Institute, May 5, 1997. Reprinted by permission.

As you read, consider the following questions:

1. Should there be a limit to campaign donations by an individual to a candidate? Why or why not?
2. Is the FECA still relevant to current elections? Why or why not?
3. What are the drawbacks to longer lengths of electoral campaigns?

[…]

I think it is important to note up front that, except for a brief period of less than five years in the mid-1970s, unlimited contributions and spending of what we now call "soft money" have always been lawful in the United States. (In fact, it is unclear that Congress intended to ban "soft money" contributions even in the 1970s, and soft money contributions were soon reauthorized, first through regulatory interpretation and later by express act of Congress.) So to suggest a complete ban on soft money, as some have done, or sharp limits on soft money, as proposed by S. 25 (the "McCain-Feingold bill"), is, in fact, quite a radical departure from our historic system of democratic elections.

[…]

In addition to grassroots campaign activity, soft money also funds voter registration drives, phone banks, and get-out-the-vote efforts conducted by parties. I think that there can be little doubt that drying up the source of money for such activities will accelerate the decline in voter turnout—a decline which, I emphasize, has increased since we began to heavily regulate campaign spending and contributions in 1974. Absent the soft money "loophole," parties could not undertake voter registration and get-out-the-vote drives because these activities can benefit candidates for federal office, and thus would count as contributions in excess of the amounts allowed under FECA. Thus, Congress should approach the issue of soft money contributions carefully. Soft money serves a number of valuable purposes in the political system.

[...]

The Supreme Court has correctly recognized that limits on campaign contributions and spending have the effect of directly limiting political speech. For that reason, the Court has struck down mandatory limits on campaign spending, *Buckley v. Valeo*, 424 US 1 (1976). The presidential campaign system of tax dollar funding is constitutional only because it is voluntary: candidates agree to limit their spending in return for limited government financing of their campaigns.

However, the Court also held in *Buckley* that limits on independent expenditures, that is, expenditures made independently of a candidate's campaign, are unconstitutional. This is because expenditures, if truly independent of the campaign, have little potential for corruption. This would seem to be especially true of expenditures made by parties in support of their own candidates, and last year, in *Colorado Republican Federal Campaign Committee v. Federal Election Commission*, 116 S.Ct.2309, the Court ruled that political parties had a constitutional right to make independent expenditures. Thus, if party expenditures are made independently of the candidate's campaign, they cannot be limited by Congress. However, if expenditures by parties cannot be limited, can the size of the contributions to the parties be limited?

[...]

The difficulty of attempting to limit soft money contributions is that soft money is, by definition, spent on activities that lie outside the permissive scope of regulation as determined by *Buckley*. That is to say, soft money expenditures do not go for direct advocacy in support of a candidate. Even the type of television advertisements featuring party candidates, described above, do not include the express words of advocacy, such as "elect" or "defeat," which would allow them to be regulated under the First Amendment. And, of course, bills such as S. 25 particularly single out and ban soft money party expenditures on get-out-the-vote drives, voter registration drives, and any generic party activity that might affect a federal race (S. 25, Sec. 325 et seq.). This is not only of questionable constitutionality, but is also ridiculously poor public policy.

[…]

Many are frustrated that the First Amendment limits our ability to silence certain voices that they feel "distort" or "corrupt" our political campaigns. But the Constitutional limits on regulating candidate and independent expenditures, campaign and soft money contributions, and "issue advocacy," are no more "loopholes" than the Fourth Amendment prohibition on unreasonable searches and seizures is a "loophole" in the fight against crime. I have little doubt that we could catch more criminals if we could dispense with search warrants, but we realize that that cannot be done consistent with the Fourth Amendment and the protection of our liberties. Few liberties can be more important than the right to engage in political speech, and Congress must tread with great caution in this area. Congress should stop trying to "get around" First Amendment limits on regulating political speech. Only by abandoning such unconstitutional schemes to police political speech, can we gain a new perspective on the issues, and begin to seriously address some of the problems in modern presidential campaigns.

[…]

At the federal level, as I'm sure the members of this Committee know all too well, contributions to campaigns are limited to $1000 in the case of individuals, and to $5000 in the case of political action committees, or PACs. At the presidential level, candidates have the option of receiving federal matching funds in the primaries, and federal funding for the general election campaign, if they agree to certain spending limits. Let's break that system down and look at the consequences of those three major sections of the law: contribution limits; spending limits; and the public financing formula.

[…]

Consequences of FECA

Time Constraints and the Appearance of Corruption

The necessity of raising money in small contributions of $1000 or less forces representatives to spend inordinate amounts of time raising money. In modern America, approximately five percent of the electorate will make some political contribution in a two year election cycle. This may seem like a small number, but the fact is, no other system in the world enjoys such broad based financial support. This suggests the difficulty of relying on small contributors to finance campaigns. The task gets more difficult each year, eating up more of a candidate or legislator's time. Jack Kemp has likened the process of funding a campaign with $1000 contributions to that of filling a swimming pool with a teaspoon. A major reason that the low contribution limit was found constitutional in *Buckley* was the need to combat the "appearance of corruption."

[...]

Fewer Candidates

In 1996, several prominently mentioned candidates for President decided not to seek their party's nomination, including, but not limited to, General Colin Powell, former Representative Jack Kemp, and former Vice President Dan Quayle. For each, the need to devote substantial time to fund raising was cited as a major deterrent to running. Oddly enough, magazine publisher Steve Forbes, who, under the Constitution, could spend unlimited sums of his own money on his own candidacy, did run. Forbes, however, made little secret that his preference would have been to see Kemp run. Thus, in addition to diverting candidate energies to fund-raising, FECA seems to be discouraging candidacies and distorting who runs for office.

Longer Campaigns

A common complaint among the electorate is that campaigns have become too long. This is also, in part, a consequence of FECA. Because of the low fund raising limits and the corresponding time that must be spent raising funds, candidates must, as a practical matter, declare their candidacies earlier with each election. It is worth noting that in 1968, before FECA, Senator Gene McCarthy was able to launch a challenge to President Lyndon Johnson, starting just a few months before the critical New Hampshire primary. He was able to do this because he was able to raise the necessary funds in a very short period of time, getting large, six figure contributions from Stewart Mott, Jack Dreyfuss, and a handful of others. Under FECA, it would be next to impossible for a candidate to launch such a late starting campaign, unless, like Ross Perot or Steve Forbes, the candidate was a multi-millionaire capable of funding his or her own campaign.

Stifling New Ideas

It is often suggested that campaigns have become bereft of new ideas. This can be attributed in part to low contribution limits. To raise campaign funds in small contributions, a candidate must appeal to a large number of donors from the very start of the campaign. This means that the candidate will generally adopt positions on issues which are non-controversial or already quite popular. Absent restrictions on the size of contributions, candidates, supported only by a small group of committed citizens, might be able to raise the money and take their case for new or controversial solutions to the citizenry. However, when contributions are limited, a candidate cannot raise the funds to campaign without beginning with broad appeal; this leads to the adoption of superficial policies and solutions. Candidates who seek to lead, rather than follow, or who stake out bold positions on issues, are deprived of the necessary funds to take their case to the people, and so placed at a competitive disadvantage. In the last two presidential elections, the candidates who have brought new ideas to the public were two maverick millionaires, Ross Perot and Steve Forbes. It does not really matter, for our purposes today, what any of us think of the policies they proposed. What I want to point out is that they put issues on the agenda that none of the traditional candidates was discussing, and they were able to do so only because they could spend unlimited personal sums on their campaigns. Milquetoast campaigns do not help voter turn-out, and, because controversial issues are ignored, they have a tendency to deteriorate into personal, negative campaigns, aimed at tearing down the opposition while doing and saying nothing controversial about any issue. If personal attacks seem to have replaced ideas in modern campaigns, contribution limits are certainly a contributing factor to that trend.

[...]

Consequences of Campaign Spending Limits

S. 25 makes a feeble effort to overcome this by giving Senate candidates an added allowance if they face primary opposition. This fails to take into account the nature of opposition, or the different strengths and weaknesses of the candidate. Indeed, under S. 25, a candidate without primary opposition should have his campaign director run against him in the primary, thus triggering an added spending allowance. Of course, the campaign director's competing campaign might be less than effective: it might even be run so incompetently that it would seem to help his opponent.

Similarly, S. 25 allows a candidate to exceed the spending limits in order to counter independent expenditures made against the candidate. This could also lead to interesting results. For example, a clever, pro-Democratic group might runs advertisements "supporting" GOP candidate Jones. The ads, targeted at senior citizens, might say, "Candidate Jones wants to cut Medicare and Medicaid spending. Isn't it about time we had a Senator with the courage to say 'no' to the greedy seniors' lobbyists? Vote Jones!" Not only would this ad probably help Jones' opponent directly, but it would then allow that opponent to spend more money in order to "counter" these independent expenditures.

[...]

Dishonest Campaigns

Spending limits tend to create dishonest campaigns, which reduces accountability and adds to voter cynicism. I have just given two examples of how spending limits can be circumvented by dishonest campaigning. And, of course, we saw that in the issue ads that the parties ran supporting their presidential nominees last year, ads which nevertheless stopped short of exhorting voters to vote for or against a particular candidate. As I have indicated, it is probably unconstitutional, and in my view bad policy, to attempt to ban such ads.

What we see then, is the inevitable result of attempting to limit the participation of citizens in politics. A member of this committee was quite right when he described such efforts as "putting a rock on jello." People have a right to participate in political activity, and will find ways to do so. Limiting direct participation merely forces activity into indirect channels, which is more harmful, just as a dammed river creates more problems when it overflows its banks than when allowed to follow its natural course.

Consequences of the Existing Funding Formula for Presidential Campaigns

The existing scheme for federal funding of the Presidential elections has a number of particular defects, some of which relate the particulars of the system, and others which would be endemic to any effort to design a public financing scheme.

[…]

The first is the state by state limits included in the system. A candidate seeking his party's nomination is subject not only to total spending limits, but to limits in each state. This inhibits the ability of candidates to structure their campaigns to their maximum benefit, and leads to inefficient use of resources as candidates attempt to get around the state by state limits. For example, candidates in the crucial New Hampshire primary will often rent cars in Massachusetts and drive them to New Hampshire for use there.

Thus, the cost of the cars is assessed against the Massachusetts spending limit, stretching the New Hampshire budget.

[...]

Leveraging Contributions

The matching funds formula artificially assists those candidates whose average qualifying contribution is highest. For example, in 1992, the average qualifying contribution to Lyndon LaRouche was $179, meaning that for each contribution, LaRouche received an average of $179 in federal matching funds. Bill Clinton's average qualifying contribution that year, however, was just $75, and George Bush's just $76. Thus, for each qualifying contribution, LaRouche received twice as much in matching funds as Clinton or Bush. It should be obvious by now that I greatly discount the importance of attempting to artificially assure that each candidate has the same resources. However, I see no reason at all why the federal government, if it feels it must subsidize campaigns, should do so in a manner that actually penalizes candidates who rely on smaller donations.

[...]

Discrimination Against Minor Parties

Even as public funding forces taxpayers to subsidize the pre-nomination campaigns of candidates such as LaRouche, it discriminates against third party efforts. A new party is not eligible for federal funds for the general election unless it polled at least five percent of the vote in the last general election. (All of the candidates I just mentioned received their federal funds while pursuing their parties' nominations.) If it did not, it gets no federal funds before the next general election. However, if it polls over five percent in that election, it may be eligible, retroactively, for federal funds. The problem is that the candidate needs the money to fund the campaign before the election. In fact, even significant third party candidates such as John Anderson in 1980 have found it all but impossible to borrow money before the general election, on the assumption that the candidate will draw five percent of the vote and pay the loan back with federal funds after the election. This would be a tolerable situation if new parties were not hamstrung by the same fund raising restrictions as the Republicans and Democrats. However, they labor under the same difficulty of raising money in amounts of $1000 or less, with no offsetting federal funds to relieve the burden.

[…]

Conclusion

The system of Presidential funding points up the shortcoming of any effort to limit the amount that candidates and individuals can spend on politics. The purpose of campaigns is to discuss issues and candidates. Citizens have a desire, and a constitutional right, to participate in politics: and as the Supreme Court has recognized, virtually every method of political communication requires individuals to spend money. There are some in this Congress who can't help but see the First Amendment as a "loophole" to their desire to ban or limit private participation in political discussion. Soft money is merely their most prominent target. Their goals cannot, I believe, be realized in a manner consistent with the Constitution.

[…]

| "*Who is doing the spending? And who is responsible for it?*"

Private Financing Can Result in Blurred Messaging

Matt Motyl

In the following viewpoint Matt Motyl details the common conception that money is the most important aspect of politics, even going back to the earliest days of the United States' government. Primarily, this viewpoint details the growth of Super PACs since the 2010 Citizens United Decision and how these organizations further obscure the public's ability to truly understand who is behind the funding of major party candidates in major elections. The author also argues that, because there are regulations against candidates coordinating with Super PACs, there is no way for a candidate to ensure that the Super PAC run messages to the public that are truly in line with the candidate's electoral platform. Motyl is executive director of Civil Politics, a non-profit organization that is run by academics who use data to understand moral psychology.

As you read, consider the following questions:

1. What has made it possible for just .05% of the American population to determine candidates for a federal election?
2. What can campaign finance regulation do to address public concerns of campaign advertising by *Super PACs*?
3. How has *Citizens United* impacted the growth of *Super PACs* and what should be done to regulate them?

A s Senator Mark Hanna said in 1895: "There are two things that are important in politics. The first is money and I can't remember what the second one is." The need to raise vast sums of money from special interests drives the behavior of elected officials in many ways, most of them bad for civility and public policy. Here, for example, is a list of the "heavy hitters," the biggest donors to congressional campaigns, according to FEC records.

In this TEDtalk Lawrence Lessing notes that big funders representing a mere .05% of the population are able to determine the pool of possible candidates in federal elections. According to Lessig we are no longer living in a democracy that's truly representative. His solution is to institute small donor funding. But even if such a feat could be achieved it's far from clear that it would ameliorate the hyperpartisan divide that fuels so much incivility and bad faith.

If we're trying to find examples of civil political discourse, election campaigns probably wouldn't be the first place we'd think to look. Campaigns are, after all, fundamentally adversarial in nature. And American political history is littered with invective to show it. Bringing the mudslinging of the past into a modern form, these parody ads suggest that the election of 1800, at least, was hardly a paragon of civility! But modern communication brings attack politics to the masses with greater personal immediacy, and on a vast scale.

Negative ads are not entirely negative, of course. On the most basic level, the fact is that they work. They tap into a more general psychological finding that bad is often stronger than good, as people pay more attention to negative information (this is known as negativity bias). Moreover, political scientists have found that negative ads can help to mobilize voters. This may be bad for some candidates, but greater participation is an important democratic value. Nonetheless, negative advertising also breeds cynicism, lower feelings of citizen efficacy, and diminishes public trust in government, thus putting broader democratic values at risk.

So how do we go about addressing these concerns? Many people point to campaign finance regulation. Television advertising, of course, is expensive, and so restricting money in elections is seen as a way to control some of the ill-effects of negative advertising—helping to cut it off at the source. The emergence of *Super PACs* in the wake of the 2010 Citizens United decision, and their heavy spending on negative advertising, has also increased scrutiny of campaign finance law in this regard. Considering the four main *Super PACs* supporting remaining GOP candidates, for example, approximately 77% of their ads have been negative. But as a means of communicating with voters, money spent on advertising is viewed as constitutionally protected speech. Altering this situation through campaign finance reform alone is thus far from straightforward.

The Legal Context

Campaign finance laws can certainly shape the nature and extent of public discourse, with the *Super PAC* example only the latest example of this.

Setting disclosure requirements aside for the moment, the campaign finance regime is, at its heart, a series of tradeoffs for political actors—between the amount of money you can raise and spend, how explicitly your communications can advocate for or against a candidate, and how much you can coordinate that activity with a candidate or party. In essence, the less you coordinate, the less restricted your fundraising and spending, and the more you can advocate.

Political Financing for Women

Money is essential for the operations of political parties, and particularly affects candidates in electoral processes. Political financing regulations can effect women's access to run as candidates, be elected, campaign and reach out to the population. Regulations on political funding are used to level the playing field in electoral competition. They can also work to ensure that women are able to compete on a more equal footing with men. This in turn may result in women's increased political participation; a key feature of democracy.

Funding regulations need to be context specific and respond the realities on the ground. iKNOW Politics is seeking to collect information on laws, regulations or practices that have been put in place to address challenges women face in raising money in politics. We would like to know about good experiences in this area, in particular related to the following questions:

- Are there formal (legislated) mechanisms that work to level the (financial) playing field between women and men candidates? If so, what are they (e.g. spending limits, campaigning time limits, disclosure, reforms to public funding that may benefit women)?
- Are there adverse effects for women candidates in the existing laws on political finance? What can be changed, or what provisions could be strengthened (e.g. ensuring enforcement of campaign finance regulations, including disclosure; prohibition of illicit funding)? Are there any controls in place?
- How have political parties addressed the gender funding gap (e.g. voluntary—not legislated—practices such as internal fundraising mechanisms, in-kind contributions for campaigns)? If so, what are they?
- Are there differences in how women and men candidates spend their campaign funds? E.g. higher spending for women due to lack of security, childcare costs, etc.

"Political Financing for Women," iKNOW Politics.

This configuration emerged out of a 1976 Supreme Court decision. Examining major campaign finance reforms passed in the early 1970s which placed caps on contributions to campaigns but also various types of spending, the Court ruled that spending made "independently" of a candidate or party (i.e. not coordinated with them) could not be regulated (on grounds of free speech) —either in terms of the amounts raised/spent or the nature of communications funded. Thus individuals and unincorporated associations were free to make "independent expenditures" in campaigns, but corporations and labor unions were still restricted in this regard—due to a separate prohibition on their political activities contained elsewhere in the law. *Citizens United* basically removed that prohibition—corporations and labor unions can now make independent expenditures (though they are still restricted in other ways, such as being unable to make direct donations to candidates). *Super PACs* emerged from subsequent court and FEC decisions that extended this reasoning—if an individual corporation can make independent expenditures, then they can also get together to do the same.

So how does this affect political discourse?

The concerns raised by independent expenditures are made more concrete when we think about electoral spending by "outside groups." When spending isn't coming from the candidate's campaign or the party—actors we can readily identify and whose contributors are strictly regulated—two main questions emerge: who is doing the spending? And who is responsible for it? These generate interrelated concerns about accountability and anonymity —both of which can lead to greater negativity in political discourse.

Accountability: When questioned about *Super PAC* attacks ads during the South Carolina Republican primary debate, for example, Mitt Romney responded, "the *Super PACs* run ads, and if they ever run an ad or say something that's not accurate, I hope that they either take off the ad or make it correct." But due to the legal prohibition on coordination, Romney can have no active role in ensuring this happens. And this lack of control—and lack of accountability—can also affect the tone of campaigns. While the ads aired by the four main candidate *Super PACs* are about 77% negative, as noted above, about 54% of those aired by the candidate campaigns themselves are negative.

This difference raises an important concern about *Super PACs*, or other "outside groups" like 527s, 501(c) organizations, or unincorporated associations—that they might make accusations and attacks that candidates would not be willing to make themselves. In the current GOP primary contest, for example, Newt Gingrich, may have benefited from a film critiquing Romney's career at Bain Capital, even as he called for the film to be edited.

A congressional committee chaired by Fred Thompson investigating campaign finance in 1997 came to just this conclusion —considering an earlier wave of advertising. And despite requirements in the Bipartisan Campaign Reform Act of 2002 (BCRA) that candidates appear in—and take direct responsibility for—their own ads, we don't seem any further along as regards outside groups.

Anonymity: A second concern relates anonymity—who is doing the spending. On one level, outside groups are often given universalist, patriotic names that make it hard to identify the interests or individuals that may be involved—even when the group itself is identified in an ad. A particular concern with *Super PACs*, moreover, is that it can be impossible to identify some of the individual donors at all.

Like regular PACs, *Super PACs* do have to report to the FEC, but because *Citizens United* also freed non-profit corporations —like the Chamber of Commerce—to engage in unlimited independent expenditures, and because such entities only face minimal disclosure regulation from the IRS, it is possible to funnel money into *Super PACs* without having to disclose the identity of original donor. We all know that people are more willing to be critical of someone else, if they think it won't be traced back to them. Indeed, anonymity has even been linked to aggression in lab studies. Unsurprisingly then, the kinds of organizational and individual anonymity we see in *Super PACs* can lead to less civil discourse.

Solutions?

Some of these concerns could be mitigated by more stringent disclosure provisions. The DISCLOSE Act, for example, can help individuals to trace where money is coming from, and thus hold people more accountable for the incivility they may create. In addition, work by the Sunlight Foundation has the potential for reducing incivility by increasing the transparency of political actors.

But it's harder to turn the clock back on some of the organizational developments. As political scientist Ray La Raja has recently argued, by placing restrictions on candidate campaigns and, especially, political party organizations—campaign finance laws have actually encouraged the growth of outside groups— groups which are then difficult to control without running afoul of free speech protections. He suggests substantially increasing the limits on contributions to parties and candidate campaigns so as to concentrate more activity within these "inside" groups. And it's almost impossible to place restrictions on the nature of speech, as opposed to limiting its extent—so it's difficult to legislate our way out of the problem of negative advertising.

This means that individual efforts to alter the way we think about, and speak about, political opponents are incredibly important. And by improving how we talk about people in campaigns—the arena in which incivility is most likely to occur —such efforts can have a positive impact across the political system.

> *"The next question is one of logistics: can public funding be adapted to work on the national scale in today's tumultuous campaign finance environment?"*

How Do We Fix Campaign Finance?

Sanoja Bhaumik

In the following viewpoint, Sanoja Bhaumik describes the questions surrounding campaign finance reform. The author explores the question of whether Americans have the right to make the changes that will allow them to support candidates in a truly democratic process. Bhaumik describes the processes in other democratic countries, including France, which has strict limits on electoral contributions and a majority of its elections are paid for with public funds, which places all the candidates on equal footings. Bhaumik argues that the United States has the Federal Election Campaign Act of 1976, which put federal funds in place for elections, but is still irrelevant for many candidates. Bhaumik is a writer and graduate of Yale University.

As you read, consider the following questions:

1. What is the theory behind implementing public funding on a national scale in the United States? Is it viable? Why or why not?
2. Is public funding the future of campaign finance reform in the United States? Why or why not?
3. How does the FECA of 1976 differ from elections that are publicly funded as a whole?

In the upcoming 2016 election, campaign finance is quickly becoming a campaign issue. Donald Trump has repeatedly brought voters amusing images of his fellow Republican candidates begging the Koch brothers for donations. On the other side of the aisle, Bernie Sanders has made headlines by denying money from *Super PACs* and still raising $26 million through grassroots support. While the national conversation about campaign finance is loud and contentious, it lacks a global perspective. We are neither the first nation to face this challenge, nor will we be the last.

Nations around the world have found varied and distinct ways to respond to money in politics. Countries such as France, Canada, and Japan have stringent spending and contribution limits to prevent outside influences in elections. Sophie Menard '19, who grew up in Paris, said in contrast to private donations, public funding makes up the majority of France's campaign finance system. She said, "The state gives a set amount of money for candidates so that candidates are on equal footing from the start."

This concept of public funding is all but foreign to the United States. The Federal Election Campaign Act (FECA) of 1976 put federal public funds in place, and presidential candidates have used public funds in every election cycle from 1976 to 2008. In recent years, however, due to the enormous number of funds needed to run an effective campaign, the small amount provided by the bill border on irrelevancy to presentday candidates. The dwindling influence of FECA is evidenced by the fact that the

2012 presidential election was the first since the start of the program in which no public funds were spent. Many, including Richard Briffault, a professor at Columbia Law School and Chair of the Conflicts of Interest Board of the City of New York, believe that national public funding could be revived if more funds were given to the system to allow candidates to run an effective campaign without relying on large private donors. The question still remains: is public funding a desirable solution?

In contrast to the national scale, local public funding programs in the United States have continued to be relevant today. New York City's matching funds program, established in 1988, has been cited as highly successful by proponents of a nationally scaled program due to its candidate participation rate of 90 percent. Participating candidates receive six dollars from the city for every one dollar a private donor contributes, with the condition that they adhere to strict contribution limits. But in an interview with The Politic, Bradley Smith, Chairman of the Federal Election Commission from 2000 to 2005, criticized the system. "Although it works in the sense that it garners candidate participation, the public funding does not lead to better governance," he said. He cited New York City's "high rate of government corruption, one-party politics, and high rate of incumbency," adding that campaign finance reform must be examined for its "meaningful effects and changes in government" rather than for its success as a separate system.

Richard Briffault, on the other hand, believes that public funding brings about the meaningful change to which Smith alludes. He told The Politic, "The success of public funding is not seen in the competitiveness of elections, but rather in the contestation of elections. In state legislature elections without public funding, there is rarely even another candidate. When public funding is introduced, that tends to end." In elections with public funding, such as those held in New York City, Briffault argued, "Incumbents don't lose less, but they are contested. This contestation forces incumbents, even if they win, to be more responsive to their constituents." He also argued that public funding makes it possible

CRITICISMS OF THE FEDERAL ELECTION CAMPAIGN ACT

Critics argue that FECA strengthens the domination of the two major political parties. By limiting an individual's direct contributions to a candidate, the act prevents minor parties from amassing enough funds to gain ground on the two major parties. The Democratic and Republican parties can survive such limitations because they have large numbers of contributors. According to some critics, they have large numbers of contributors because they have the power to give political favors. Minor parties, by definition, begin their missions with fewer supporters and have no political favors to bestow. With contribution limits on their few supporters, minor parties have few opportunities to mount serious challenges to the major-party candidates.

Other critics of FECA focus on the reporting and bookkeeping responsibilities required by the act and the sheer complexity of the law. Minor parties, with their meager funds, have difficulty in managing the detailed records and reporting requirements, and in paying for the legal assistance that they need in order to comply with the law. By comparison, major parties possess enough experience and support staff to surmount the demands of the act.

"Soft" money is another concern for critics of FECA. In the context of political campaigns, soft money is cash that is given to a political party, not directly to a candidate. There is no limit to the amount that a person or organization may give to a political party. Political parties may use the contributions that they receive to benefit themselves generally; they may not use those contributions to benefit one particular candidate. There are, however, effective detours around this roadblock. For example, a party may run a television advertisement that criticizes the opponent of a particular candidate. The money spent by the party on such a commercial will not be listed as a direct contribution to the party's candidate if the advertisement does not mention the party's own candidate. Major-party candidates, with this kind of help from the national and state committees of their party, benefit from this practice more frequently than do minor-party candidates.

"Election Campaign Financing Private Funding of Federal Election Campaigns," http://law.jrank.org/pages/6374.

for more New Yorkers to run for office. "Neighborhood candidates are able to run due to New York's generous 6:1 funding ratio. The higher turnover rate among elected officials is even greater evidence of a more democratic system."

The Brennan Center for Justice, a thinktank based in New York University Law School that focuses on democracy and justice, echoed Briffault's views. According to a 2012 study commissioned by the Center, public funding increases political participation among citizens: 90% of census block groups in New York City contained small donors, many representing low-income minority areas. This trend is rare in most elections; in New York State legislature elections, only 30% of census block groups had small donors.

The next question is one of logistics: can public funding be adapted to work on the national scale in today's tumultuous campaign finance environment? According to Briffault, in theory, it can. "Public funding could work in the US on a national scale because it has worked before." He pointed to the "six electoral cycles from 19761992 in which public funds played a large role in presidential elections." However, because FECA only offered public funding in presidential elections, Briffault cited many new obstacles that could hinder the application of such a program in congressional elections. "What level of funding ought to be?" he asked. He alluded to the fact that some congressional district elections require much more money than others in order to fund a competitive campaign and questioned how the government would reconcile these variances among districts. Additionally, the US faces an obstacle that many Western countries do not: competitive primaries. Briffault said, "Most western countries have party elections as opposed to candidate elections. In the US, the primary is the most competitive election in many districts."

The International Institute for Democracy and Electoral Assistance (IIDEA) has also reported that lax contribution limits in many western countries, including Denmark, Sweden, and Germany, exist because of strong party politics and discipline in parliamentary forms of government. In addition, according to IIDEA, limits in many Western countries occur in other forms, such as Denmark's complete ban on television advertisements, the single largest cost of campaigns in the US Briffault also explained, "Limits in these forms [including limiting election campaign seasons or banning certain forms of advertising] would be virtually impossible in the US due to *Citizens United* and First Amendment rights." Bradley Smith, the former FEC Chairman, agrees with this reasoning, citing "the unique political situation in the United States, that on top of our vibrant rights, we adhere to explicit rights and frameworks outlined in the Constitution."

Expanding on the question of constitutionality and whether or not the policies of other countries would fit those of the United States, Smith said the first and only requirement of any campaign finance limit is that it fit the tenets of the constitution. "If new policies are in place, they must adhere to the First Amendment specifically, which gives the right of Americans to participate and donate to political campaigns as they desire," he said. Briffault, on the other hand, believes in more flexibility. He said, "The First Amendment has limitations with good justifications…. Campaign spending does implicate the first amendment, [but] protecting democracy and the right to vote justifies limitations."

Nevertheless, considering the restrictions of campaign finance reform in the wake of *Citizens United v. FEC*, Briffault cited "the need of levelup campaign finance policies," using tactics such as increasing voter registration and using public funding to force candidates to listen to their constituents. The landmark court case ruled in favor of unlimited contributions and led to the creation of billion dollar *Super PACs* in the 2012 Presidential election. Briffault emphasized that in order to adhere to the policy restrictions put in place by *Citizens United*, lawmakers need to rethink the traditional forms of campaign finance, such as contribution limits, and suggested that expanding public funding could be the solution. He does, however, credit the US campaign finance system for its uniquely stringent disclosure requirements compared to other western countries, which force candidates to reveal who funds their campaigns. Smith also agreed with this statement, explaining that other countries, such as France, tend to view disclosure as a privacy harm whereas the United States views it as necessary to democracy. The strong disclosure laws already in place could strengthen a renewed national public funding program.

The question of what to do with campaign finance reform lies in what we want our country to be, and where we want these changes to lead. Do we, as Americans, have the right to support our candidates in a democratic process? Does our right infringe on others? Can public funding be revived in a political climate with unpredictable changes in campaign spending? These questions must be answered by our presidential candidates as they struggle to balance constitutionality and equal representation. But if international trends or even our past policies are any indication, public funding could be the future of campaign finance reform in the US.

> "Most of the countries in the OECD
> have traditions of stricter party
> discipline than we do, and that
> makes members of the legislature
> somewhat interchangeable."

The US Has Different Priorities Than Other Countries When It Comes to Campaign Rules

Paul Waldman

In the following viewpoint, Paul Waldman examines the similarities and differences of the United States' campaign finance system, compared to other countries around the world. Using information from the International Institute for Democracy and Electoral Assistance (International IDEA) and placing an emphasis on nations that are members of the Organisation for Economic Cooperation and Development (OECD), Waldman breaks it down into four categories: the No-Limits nations, which include Australia, Germany, Spain, Switzerland; the All-Limit nations, which include Canada, France, Greece, Israel, Japan; the nations with limits on spending but not on donations: Austria, Italy, New Zealand, the United Kingdom; and nations with contribution limits, but no spending limits: Finland, the United States. Waldman is a weekly columnist and senior writer for The American Prospect.

"How Our Campaign Finance System Compares to Other Countries," by Paul Waldman, Prospect.org, April 4, 2014.

As you read, consider the following questions:

1. Why is TV advertising not a large expense in countries outside of the United States?
2. What is the difference between a limit on spending and a limit on donations?
3. Which countries' elections benefit the most from their regulations?

With the Supreme Court's decision in the McCutcheon case, some people think we're heading for the complete removal of contribution limits from campaigns. Jeffrey Toobin, for instance, argues that the way Justice Roberts defines corruption—basically, nothing short of outright bribery qualifies—means that he could well be teeing things up to eliminate contribution limits entirely in some future case. Which got me thinking: if we really are headed for that eventual outcome, how would that place us compared to other countries? For instance, if you're a Monsieur Koch in France, can you write a candidate a million-euro check?

Fortunately, the good folks at the International Institute for Democracy and Electoral Assistance (International IDEA), an inter-governmental agency, have gathered this kind of information together. Of course, a large database of laws from all over the world is going to miss many of the subtleties and loopholes that characterize each individual country's system. But if you were thinking that other similarly advanced democracies must all have tighter laws than ours, you wouldn't be exactly right.

While International IDEA's database contains information on 43 variables for 172 countries, for the moment I decided to focus on two questions: Are there limits on contributions to parliamentary candidates, and are there limits on spending? I also decided to focus on the 34 member nations of the Organisation for Economic Cooperation and Development, since the OECD is how we often define "countries like us." And I eliminated Mexico and Portugal, where all contributions go through parties and individual candidates don't take contributions. So, what does the picture look like?

The No-Limits Nations: Australia, the Czech Republic, Denmark, Estonia, Germany, Luxembourg, the Netherlands, Norway, Spain, Sweden, Switzerland, and Turkey.

In these places, there are no limits on contributions, and no limits on what candidates can spend. But that doesn't mean that these countries' wealthy are writing million-euro checks to parliamentary candidates. It's important to keep in mind that the role money is able to play in politics is determined by multiple factors, many of which serve to hold down both contributions and spending, even when the law doesn't impose limits. For instance, most of the countries in the OECD have traditions of stricter party discipline than we do, and that makes members of the legislature somewhat interchangeable, which in turn can reduce the utility of buying yourself a few of them. Even more importantly, TV advertising is the single largest expense for most American congressional candidates, while in many other countries candidates are either forbidden from advertising on television or given free TV time. In most places there's substantial public funding of campaigns, and candidates are often forbidden from campaigning until a relatively short period before election day. Put all that together, and you have elections where, even if it would technically be legal to rain huge amounts of money down on candidates, nobody considers it worth their while (for instance, here's a nice description of the relative quiet of a German campaign). So the idea of someone spending two or three million dollars to get a seat in the national legislature, the way American House candidates routinely do, would seem absurd.

The All-Limit Nations: Belgium, Canada, Chile, France, Greece, Iceland, Ireland, Israel, Japan, South Korea, Poland, Slovenia.

In these countries, there are limits on both contributions and on spending. The contribution limits tend to be in the same rough ballpark as ours (the current limit for US federal campaigns is $2,600 in the primary and $2,600 in the general). So in Canada, you can give $1,100 to a parliamentary candidate; in Greece it's $3,000 euros, in Iceland it's a little under $2,500 euros, and so on. There are a couple of outliers—in Japan, you can contribute 1.5 million yen, or $14,439 in today's exchange rate, to each candidate per year. Another is Israel, where a complicated formula will allow you to contribute a couple of hundred thousand dollars to some candidates.

But spending limits, which are quite low in most places (often in the five figures), make all the difference. Which brings us to:

The Nations with Limits on Spending but Not on Donations: Austria, Hungary, Italy, New Zealand, Slovakia, the United Kingdom.

It does seem a little odd that you would have limits on what a parliamentary candidate can spend, but no limits on what someone can donate to her. But if you have the former, you don't really need the latter. If a candidate is only allowed to spend $20,000, she doesn't really have to worry about seeking out donations (a raffle or two down at the pub might do the trick), and there's no point in writing her a big check to try to win her favor. And finally...

The Nations with Contribution Limits but No Spending Limits: Finland, the United States.

Not knowing much about Finnish elections, I'm not going to speak to what goes on there (though if I had to guess I'd say they're polite, thoughtful affairs). But for American candidates, it's the worst of both worlds. The lack of spending limits means they're always at risk of being outspent, which means they can never stop raising money. But the lack of contribution limits means they have to get that money in $2,600 increments, meaning they have to keep asking and asking and asking.

If we removed the contribution limits, it would certainly make candidates' lives easier; if you can convince one billionaire to write you a check for $2.6 million, that's the equivalent of persuading a thousand ordinarily reach people to give you $2,600, and that would free you up to spend a lot more time calling your opponent a low-down cur who wants to bring the republic to ruin. But would it make the system more corrupt? You bet it would.

As you look over the different regulations various countries have come up with, it does seem that the thing that makes all the difference in how campaigns are conducted is the spending limits, which are often combined with time limits on electioneering. Everyone has to weigh two competing considerations. The first is the desire for elections that retain a reasonable amount of integrity, and are conducted in a manner that is, for lack of a better term, civilized. And the second is the principle of free speech, that a candidate for office should be able to say what he wants, as often as he wants, and spend as much as he wants doing it, even at the risk of corruption. In most other countries, they've decided that the first consideration is more important. In the US, we've decided that the second consideration is the only one that matters.

Periodical and Internet Sources Bibliography

The following articles have been selected to supplement the diverse views presented in this chapter.

Lolita Cigane and Magnus Ohman, "Political Finance and Gender Equality," National Democratic Institute, August 2014. https://www.ifes.org/sites/default/files/political_finance_and_gender_equality.pdf.

Helen Drinan, "What does the Presidential election mean for gender equality?" Huffington Post, November 9, 2017. https://www.huffingtonpost.com/helen-drinan/what-does-the-presidentia_b_12867628.html.

Ken Goldstein and Paul Freedman, "Campaign Advertising and Voter Turnout: New Evidence for a Stimulation Effect," Wiley Online Library, January 23, 2003. https://www.journals.uchicago.edu/doi/10.1111/0022-3816.00143.

Michael Scott Hill, "Campaign Length and its Impact on Voter Turnout," IUPUI ScholarWorks, 2017. https://scholarworks.iupui.edu/bitstream/handle/1805/14660/Michael_Hill%20Thesis.pdf?sequence=4.

Daniel Houser, Rebecca Morton and Thomas Stratmann, "Turned on or turned out? Campaign advertising, information and voting", European Journal of Political Economy, June 3, 1999. https://pdfs.semanticscholar.org/c649/4bd24bc0b4c9d29afee55e893ebdd8bcadf4.pdf.

"How to Approach Fundraising in 2018," AFP, January 31, 2018. http://afpcoastalgeorgia.afpnet.org/International/PPIssuedetail.cfm?ItemNumber=48097.

Organization for Security and Co-operation in Europe, "Handbook for Monitoring Women's Participation in Elections," OSCE, July 13, 2004. https://www.osce.org/odihr/elections/13938.

Organization for Security and Co-operation in Europe, "Handbook on Promoting Women's Participation in Political Parties," OSCE, July 7, 2014. https://www.osce.org/odihr/120877.

Lynda W. Powell, "The Influence of Campaign Constributions on Legislative Policy," The Campaign Finance Institute, October 2013. http://www.cfinst.org/pdf/papers/02_Powell_Influence.pdf.

Felicia Sonmez, "Negative ads: Is it the campaigns, or the *Super PACs*? (Thursday's Trail Mix)," The Washington Post, March 22, 2012. https://www.washingtonpost.com/blogs/election-2012/post/negative-ads-is-it-the-campaigns-or-the-super-pacs-thursdays-trail-mix/2012/03/22/gIQAOf8VTS_blog.html?utm_term=.2ff21767d0d1.

Roberto Suro, "Campaign Fund Probe Winds Down," Washington Post Archive, May 30, 1999. http://www.washingtonpost.com/wp-srv/politics/special/campfin/stories/finance053099.htm.

Rick Zednik, "The 2017 Elections To Watch For Progress On Gender Equality," Huffington Post, January 10, 2017. https://www.huffingtonpost.com/entry/the-2017-elections-to-watch-for-progress-on-gender_us_5869252ee4b04d7df167d595.

Zocalo Public Square, "Do We Really Need Campaign Finance Reform?," Time.com, January 19, 2016. http://time.com/4182502/campaign-finance-reform/.

OPPOSING VIEWPOINTS® SERIES

CHAPTER 3

Do Corporate Donations Need More or Less Regulation?

Chapter Preface

While the United States is not alone in having a complicated campaign finance system, it is unique in that, while it places restrictions of how much can be contributed to a candidate, there is no limit on how much money a candidate can spend. One viewpoint describes a number of the 34 countries that participate in the Organisation for Economic Cooperation and Development (OECD) and the generalizations of their campaign finance laws. It includes No-Limits nations, All-Limit nations, nations with limits on spending but not on donations, and the category that the United States is in, and shares with the country of Finland.

Furthermore, the 2010 Supreme Court decision in *Citizens United v. Federal Election Commission* established that there is no total limit to how much money can be funneled to support a specific candidate, so long as the money does not go directly to that candidate and the organization does not coordinate with that candidate. That creates many questions and potential conflicts, of which current legislation is catching up on handling, but faces numerous roadblocks in doing so.

Breaking down the different ways in which a candidate can receive donations is incredibly complicated, although one viewpoint attempts to unravel the differences between 501(c)'s, 527s, PACs, Super PACs and the up-and-coming Super-Duper PACs, all of which are ways that candidates can solicit donations outside the current individual donation limits, which in 2018 stands at a maximum of $2,700 per election to a federal candidate or the candidate's campaign committee.

Using examples from countries outside the United States that face similar campaign finance issues—including Australia, which unlike the United States, has no limits to how much a candidate can either receive or spend—the following chapter includes viewpoints from contributors who focus on the status of campaign finance law in the United States and how recent Supreme Court rulings and legislation have molded it into a nebulous, difficult-to-define, and potentially corrupt system. Looking at the campaign finance models established in other countries, the question remains: Do corporate donations need more or less legislation?

*"Now, there are Super PACs—
committees that, thanks to the
court decisions, can raise and spend
unlimited sums of money from
individuals, corporations, unions
and other groups."*

Every Election Year Promises Record Spending

Kim Barker and Marian Wang

*In the following viewpoint Kim Barker and Marian Wang from
ProPublica break down the differences between 527s, Super PACs, the
up-and-coming Super-Duper PACs and other organizations that raise
funds for federal elections like 501(c)'s. In recent years, specifically
since the 2000s, there have been major changes in the ways in which
federal candidates can solicit funds for their elections. The viewpoint
shows that the January 2010 ruling in* Citizens United v. Federal
Election Commission (FEC) *opened the door for organizations to
spend unlimited money to support or criticize specific candidates, and
that the FEC has no legal power to prevent it. Barker was a reporter
at ProPublica covering "dark money" and campaign finance. Wang
was a reporter for ProPublica, covering education and college debt.*

"Super-PACs and Dark Money: ProPublica's Guide to the New World of Campaign
Finance," by Kim Barker and Marian Wang, ProPublica Inc., July 11, 2011. Reprinted by
permission.

As you read, consider the following questions:

1. When did Congress establish the FEC and why?
2. How did the McCain-Feingold law make such an impact on the current means of political donations through PACs and Super PACs?
3. What must be done to regulate organizations like PACs and Super PACs?

The nation is gearing up for yet another "most expensive election in history," the quadrennial exercise in which mind-numbing amounts of money pour into the political system. But this year promises more than just record spending—more money will be flowing from more players with more opportunities to hide the source.

Emboldened by recent court decisions, groups such as Crossroads GPS (formed by Republican strategist Karl Rove), Priorities USA (formed by former aides to President Obama) and Americans for Prosperity (formed by libertarian billionaire David Koch) have been busy raising huge sums from wealthy donors freed from old contribution limits.

The chief umpire in this game—the Federal Election Commission—is still struggling to write the rules for the hodgepodge of strange-sounding groups feeding the system. 527s? Super PACs? Even Super-Duper PACs? ProPublica decided a guide is in order.

How We Got Here

Campaign finance changed dramatically after the Watergate scandal, when Congress set up the FEC, tried to eliminate hidden donations and limited contributions to federal candidates and political action committees, or PACs.

The next major change came in 2002. The McCain-Feingold law banned political parties from collecting "soft money," or unlimited contributions from corporations, unions and others, and limited the ability of special-interest groups to run so-called "issue" ads that in reality attacked or supported candidates.

Courts and the FEC almost immediately started gnawing at the new law. And in recent years, three court decisions rolled back many of the limits on special-interest groups and potentially opened the door to foreign governments or corporations spending freely on campaigns through US corporations they control. (FEC regulations ban foreign nationals from contributing, but they say nothing about a foreign corporation donating money through a US-operated subsidiary.)

In September 2009 a federal appeals court, in *EMILY's List v. Federal Election Commission*, struck down FEC regulations and opened the door for political nonprofits like EMILY's List, which backs female Democrats who support abortion rights, to spend significantly more money on campaign activities.

In January 2010, the Supreme Court dealt a major blow to McCain-Feingold. Ruling in *Citizens United v. Federal Election Commission*, the court said that the government cannot prevent corporations and unions from spending unlimited money to support or criticize specific candidates.

Drawing on this decision in March 2010, a federal appeals court ruled in *SpeechNow.org v. Federal Election Commission* that political committees making independent expenditures—that is, spending not coordinated with or directed by a candidate's campaign—could accept donations of unlimited size.

Together, the rulings super-charged some existing fundraising groups and paved the way for new ones. The FEC, deadlocked for months on issues of disclosure and foreign money, has not yet written new rules interpreting the court decisions. That's left the field open for political strategists and lawyers.

"We're in very dangerous territory," said Fred Wertheimer, president of Democracy 21, a campaign-finance watchdog group. "There's one word to describe what's going on in the campaign-finance area: The word is 'obscene.' And it's going to result in scandal and corruption and, eventually, opportunities for reform."

Advocates say the changes are needed to protect the First Amendment rights of corporations and certain nonprofits.

"Campaign-finance laws inhibit free speech," said Sean Parnell, president of the Center for Competitive Politics, which views most campaign-finance laws as government meddling. "The First Amendment is not a guarantee that all voices will be heard as often or as effectively as all other voices. It's just a guarantee that the government won't step in and say, 'OK, you've spoken enough.'"

Super PACs: Sky's the Limit

In the old days there were just PACs—political action committees that could accept donations of up to $5,000 from individuals and pass the money along to the candidates and parties they chose.

Now, there are Super PACs—committees that, thanks to the court decisions, can raise and spend unlimited sums of money from individuals, corporations, unions and other groups. Known officially as "independent expenditure-only committees," they can't donate directly to candidates but can promote them and attack their opponents, so long as they don't coordinate with any candidate or political party.

Super PACs are still new, having debuted by spending more than $80 million on the 2010 midterm elections. Republicans pioneered the groups, but Democrats jumped in, too. Many of these new entities have innocuous-sounding names that make it hard to guess their true political intent: Concerned Taxpayers of America, Citizens for a Working America, We Love USA. (And then there's comedian Stephen Colbert's new *Super PAC*: Americans for a Better Tomorrow, Tomorrow.) More than 100 are now registered with the FEC.

Like ordinary PACs, Super PACs must disclose their donors. But because of time lags in reporting, months can go by before the identities of million-dollar donors are revealed; some weren't disclosed until after the 2010 midterm elections. Loopholes can also allow donors to stay hidden, such as when money comes from a nonprofit that doesn't have to disclose how it's funded.

Last month, the campaign-finance watchdog group Center for Responsive Politics found five Super PACs that attributed a vast majority—and in some cases all—of their funding to affiliated nonprofits that are not required to reveal donors.

Most PACs will file their first fundraising reports of the year Friday, but two Super PACs that had to file early reported raising more than $4.6 million. American Crossroads, formed by Rove to support Republican candidates, raised $3.8 million. The House Majority PAC, aimed at reclaiming the Democratic majority lost in 2010, raised $800,000.

527s: Yesterday's Super PACs

Named for the tax code governing them, "527" groups were sort of a precursor to Super PACs.

Historically, 527s had a choice—they could register as PACs and give directly to candidates under FEC limits, or they could focus on issues, allowing them to raise and spend unlimited amounts. These issue-oriented 527s were not supposed to promote or attack candidates directly, and they often focused on hot-button topics such as guns or abortion.

Strict 527 groups first played a major role in the 2004 election, blurring the line between advocating for an issue and a candidate. Three paid fines for breaking laws barring them from directly supporting or criticizing candidates.

Because of the recent court rulings, some 527s have decided to become Super-PACs so they can both raise unlimited amounts and advocate for candidates.

That said, 527 groups still played an important role in the 2010 mid-term elections, spending more than $415 million, according to the Center for Responsive Politics.

501(c)'s: The Invisibles

Also named for their section in the IRS tax code, these tax-exempt organizations include charities, civic leagues and unions. (Leave it to the IRS to make their descriptions resemble algebra homework.)

Charities that fall under the 501(c)(3) heading are not allowed to be involved in political campaigns, but other 501(c) organizations are allowed to, at least to a certain extent. That includes 501(c)(4) "social welfare" organizations, a class that includes groups like the AARP and the NAACP; 501(c)(5) labor unions, like the Teamsters; and 501(c)(6) trade associations, like the US Chamber of Commerce.

These groups could always pursue political activities while raising unlimited funds and without disclosing donors – but only if their primary purpose wasn't politics. The Sunlight Foundation described them as "perhaps the most opaque political players since pre-Watergate days of anonymous cash contributions to candidates."

The best-known of these groups is the Tea Party-supporting Americans for Prosperity, a 501(c)(4) group cofounded by billionaire David Koch, who with his brother Charles is credited with pioneering some of the bolder new campaign fundraising tactics.

Why donate anonymously, when influence is the goal? Experts say that secret giving can shield corporations from blowback when supporting controversial causes, and it can make a corporate-funded effort appear to be grassroots. Plus, no rule prevents donors from telling politicians directly about their support if it suits their needs.

"Say I gave a million dollars to Crossroads GPS," said Rick Hasen, a law professor at the University of California-Irvine who runs Election Law Blog. "You can tell the whole Republican leadership that. ProPublica can't find it, but the people you are trying to influence can find it."

So, to review: Super PACs focus only on politics but must disclose their donors. The 501(c) groups must not have politics as their primary purpose but don't have to disclose who gives them money.

But it gets even more interesting when the two groups combine powers.

Say some like-minded people form both a Super PAC and a nonprofit 501(c)(4). Corporations and individuals could then

The Importance of *Citizens United*

The *Citizens United* ruling, released in January 2010, tossed out the corporate and union ban on making independent expenditures and financing electioneering communications. It gave corporations and unions the green light to spend unlimited sums on ads and other political tools, calling for the election or defeat of individual candidates.

The decision did not affect contributions. It is still illegal for companies and labor unions to give money directly to candidates for federal office. The court said that because these funds were not being spent in coordination with a campaign, they "do not give rise to corruption or the appearance of corruption."

So if the decision was about spending, why has so much been written about contributions? For that, we need to look at another court case — *SpeechNow.org v. FEC*. The lower-court case used the Citizens United case as precedent when it said that limits on contributions to groups that make independent expenditures are unconstitutional.

And that's what led to the creation of the Super PACs, which act as shadow political parties. They accept unlimited donations from billionaires, corporations and unions and use it to buy advertising, most of it negative.

The Supreme Court kept limits on disclosure in place, and Super PACs are required to report regularly on who their donors are. The same can't be said for "social welfare" groups and some other nonprofits, like business leagues.

These groups can function the same way as Super PACs, so long as election activity is not their primary activity. But unlike the Super PACs, nonprofits do not report who funds them. That's disturbing to those who favor transparency in elections. An attempt by Congress to pass a law requiring disclosure was blocked by Republican lawmakers.

The *Citizens United* decision was surprising given the sensitivity regarding corporate and union money being used to influence a federal election. Congress first banned corporations from funding federal campaigns in 1907 with the Tillman Act. In 1947, the Taft-Hartley Act extended the ban to labor unions. But the laws were weak and tough to enforce.

"The 'Citizens United' decision and why it matters," by John Dunbar, The Center for Public Integrity, October 18, 2012.

donate as much as they want to the nonprofit, which isn't required to publicly disclose funders. The nonprofit could then donate as much as it wanted to the Super PAC, which lists the nonprofit's donation but not the original contributors.

This isn't just hypothetical. Karl Rove set up this model with the Super PAC American Crossroads and the nonprofit Crossroads GPS. While some Democrats complain about the influence of so-called "dark money," others have started to follow in his footsteps.

Now the IRS seems to be stepping in—or thinking about it. The IRS in May warned major funders of 501(c)(4) groups that their donations could be subject to gift taxes, but the agency announced last week that it would hold off on enforcement while it studies the issue.

More debate is likely. A few Democrats have already sued the FEC to try to force the disclosure of donors.

Up Next: The Super-Duper PAC?

If that's not complicated enough, several groups are pushing PACs and Super PACs into uncharted territory by creating what's been unofficially called "Super-Duper PACs." They're so new there's no agreed-upon definition—and in fact, at this point, there are at least two.

Mother Jones used the term "Super-Duper PAC" in May when reporting on a plan by Republican attorney James Bopp to recruit candidates to solicit unlimited funds for Super-PACs, which could then spend money promoting that candidate.

The FEC gave that plan the partial smackdown last month, ruling that candidates can ask donors to give to a Super-PAC, but only up to $5,000.(Probably not coincidentally, $5,000 is the most individuals can donate to PACs that give directly to candidates.)

Nonetheless, Bopp—the lawyer behind *Citizens United*—has claimed it as a victory, maintaining that the $5,000 limit is "meaningless." Why? Because though a candidate might only ask for that much, anyone could donate more.

Following their conservative counterparts, Democrats such as House Minority Leader Nancy Pelosi and Senate Majority Leader Harry Reid now have started soliciting supporters for donations to Democratic Super PACs.

Some campaign-finance watchers have referred to the "Super-Duper PAC" as a combination of a Super PAC and a traditional PAC that's not officially tied to a candidate, party, corporation, union or trade group.

Making the case for this super hybrid, the National Defense PAC, which supports Republican and Tea Party-backed veterans running for office, has sued the FEC and argued that it should be able to donate to candidates (which traditional PACs can do but *Super PACs* cannot) and raise unlimited funds for independent expenditures (which Super PACs can do but traditional PACs cannot).

A federal judge agreed, granting a preliminary injunction last month against the FEC. The judge said the two types of activities could be performed by one Super PAC—so long as the bank accounts are kept separate and the money going to directly candidates is within regular PAC contribution limits.

The matter still awaits a definitive ruling, but Dan Backer, the lawyer representing the National Defense PAC, predicts that by the end of the year, more Super PACs will be moving in this direction.

> "As soon as Labor started talking
> seriously about reform, the donations
> began to dramatically favour the
> opposition Liberals."

Political Donations Corrupt Democracy in Ways We Might Not Realize

Warwick Smith

In the following viewpoint, Warwick Smith argues that corporations view their donations as a way to ensure political access and positive consideration, even though that is not something that a corporation would claim. Additionally, Smith claims that the voting public is no longer relevant considering the donations in favor of certain interests have the ability to easily swing an election toward whatever a lobby group is working toward, whether it is less gaming regulation or machine reform. Smith points to a video by actor Russell Brand, who claims that people should not vote because it legitimizes an illegitimate system. Smith is a research economist at the progressive think tank, Per Capita.

"Political Donations Corrupt Democracy in Ways You Might Not Realise," by Warwick Smith, Guardian News and Media Limited, September 11, 2014. Reprinted by permission.

As you read, consider the following questions:

1. Why would a corporation donate similar amounts of funds to more than one political party?
2. Per the viewpoint, why did the gaming industry lobby start donating in greater amounts to the Liberals, as opposed to Labor?
3. Do Brand's claims that voting is fruitless hold water?

Corporations don't give their money away for nothing. There is an understanding (rarely made explicit) that large campaign donations buy political access and favourable consideration in policy development and legislation. Why else would a corporation, which is bound by law to pursue profits, make these donations?

Interestingly, many businesses give money to both sides of the narrow political divide; sometimes different amounts, sometimes exactly the same amount. In the lead up to the 2013 federal election in Australia, for example, Inghams gave Labor and Liberal parties each $250,000, Westfield gave them each $150,000 and ANZ gave them each $80,000. By my count, over one third of donors (excluding individuals) gave to both the coalition and Labor during 2012/13. This is not unique to Australia but occurs in all democracies, just indirectly in those places where direct political donations from corporations are illegal.

Donating equally to both sides is clearly not about helping one side win. It's an implied threat: "if you don't treat us well we'll give you less and they'll be ahead." When both major parties have the same policy on an issue, it effectively removes that issue from democratic scrutiny. This is the aim of many political donations from businesses who stand to lose from policy changes that would be popular with the electorate. Only areas of difference between contenders end up being discussion points during elections, the rest is passed over in silence.

Such a big deal is made out of the few policy differences between major parties that during campaigns they can appear to be poles apart. However, as I have discussed previously, the main contenders in developed democracies are actually very closely aligned with respect to political ideology and policy – particularly economic policy.

During their last term in office, the minority federal Labor government in Australia were more or less forced by independent MP Andrew Wilkie to attempt to implement restrictions on poker machine gambling. Prior to the discussion of reforms beginning, gaming industry lobby groups were giving similar amounts of money to both major parties but slightly favouring Labor. As soon as Labor started talking seriously about reform, the donations began to dramatically favour the opposition Liberals. The leader of the Liberal party, Tony Abbott, came out strongly against the reforms and they were eventually abandoned.

During the period in question, surveys showed that a large majority (70-75%) of Australian voters supported poker machine reform to limit the impact on problem gamblers and their families. The voters lost that one as they usually do when wealthy industries are lined up against them.

The gambling interests won the game and showed the Labor party that they weren't bluffing. If I were a gambling man, I'd put money on poker machine reform not being raised by major parties in federal politics in the near future. The gaming industry has effectively paid to have the issue taken off the national political agenda. The view of the voting public is no longer relevant.

There are many more examples of this process where corporate and other wealthy entities punish reformists by shifting financial support. The best-documented examples in recent Australian political history are the mining and carbon taxes and the Future of Financial Advice (FoFA) reforms. There has been plenty of coverage of these issues so I won't repeat the stories here.

Once a policy issue is effectively silenced, ongoing donations to both major parties help to entrench major party dominance. Large donations to both the Liberal and Labor parties further marginalise minor parties who may seek to break the silence on policy issues that the corporates or elites have purchased. In Australia, the Greens are strong advocates of poker machine reform so donations that advantage the major parties over the Greens are still worth making for corporates who want this issue out of the spotlight. When it's a two horse race, the game is relatively easy to control.

A consequence of this donation-driven approach to politics is that many areas of open political debate between and within major parties are in policy areas that the wealthy elite don't care much about, like same sex marriage or abortion, or represent divisions between corporate interests. Of course, some vestiges of ideological differences remain and show up in areas such as industrial relations and welfare.

It's clear that policy formation and the legislative agenda of major political parties is not explained simply by following money trails. However, the money trails are our best portholes into the rest of the opaque process. Who attends fundraising dinners with senior politicians that cost $10,000 a plate? What do they talk about? It's easier to spin a story to voters about why you watered down regulations than it is to tell the bankers whom you mix with socially and professionally why you couldn't help them out. Personal relationships matter to politicians as much as to the rest of us.

Sitting in the middle of this process are the lobbyists and think tanks who invent public rationalisations for policy positions that serve their clients' interests. My previous column here discussed why politicians lie. Lies are most effective when the liar believes them. The first step in effective lying is to convince ourselves of the lie. This is where the think tanks and lobbyists come in, telling politicians, for instance, that FoFA regulations have to go because compliance is onerous and damaging to the efficiency of business. Too much red tape chokes economic activity. I'm sure many in the Coalition government really believed this reason for watering down the FoFA reforms but I guarantee the idea originally came from the banks or their lobbyists who simply want to continue to rip off their customers.

This is a complex and dirty game dominated by political donations, vested interests, personal ambition, class and power. Voters are a part of the game but representing their interests may not be a politician's top priority. Politicians will only act on behalf of voters if no wealthy or powerful group objects—or if the party in question is boxed into a corner by a hung parliament or a combination of marginal electorates and strong community action.

All of this begs the question of why we should bother voting. A video of actor Russell Brand being interviewed by the BBC's Jeremy Paxman went viral last year precisely because of Brand's compelling arguments that we should not vote and that voting only legitimises a fundamentally illegitimate system. So next week, I'll follow this column up with another titled "why vote?"

> "Di Natale said corporations weren't philanthropic entities but rather donated because they expect a return on their investment."

Corporate Political Donations Are State-Sanctioned Bribery

Paul Karp

In the following viewpoint, Paul Karp details the claims made by Richard Di Natale, an Australian Senator and leader of the Australian Greens party, that corporate donations are "state-sanctioned bribery" and that he wishes to rid the Australian democracy of their "corrupting influence." Di Natale argued that state-owned enterprises should deliver things for those that use them, not just for the shareholders. He also blames the media for creating a culture that makes the public distrust the government, which Di Natale claims is how Donald Trump won the 2016 United States presidential election. Karp is a reporter for Guardian Australia.

"Corporate Political Donations Are 'State-Sanctioned Bribery', Richard Di Natale Says," by Paul Karp, Guardian News and Media Limited, March 15, 2017. Reprinted by permission.

As you read, consider the following questions:

1. Are corporate donations a way for entities to bribe the state for political rulings in their favor? Why or why not?
2. How are the Australian corporate donation issues similar and/or different from the corporate donation issues faced in the United States?
3. What can be done in both Australia and the United States to make the public more trusting of their electoral systems?

Corporate donations are "state-sanctioned bribery," Richard Di Natale has said in a speech calling for reforms to rid democracy of their "corrupting influence."

Di Natale made the comments to the National Press Club on Wednesday as well as calling for a range of progressive, state-led initiatives including a "people's bank," a four-day working week and consideration of a universal basic income.

The Greens leader said the biggest problem in Australia was not the budget deficit but the "democratic deficit."

Calling for an end to "big money politics," Di Natale said corporations weren't philanthropic entities but rather donated because they "expect a return on their investment."

"Let's just call them what they are: state-sanctioned bribery."

Di Natale derided the Coalition and Labor as the "Coles and Woolworths of politics" and said that, regardless of who won the next election, "we are going to see the big donors knocking on their doors … wanting to collect the rent."

Di Natale called for several measures including a federal anti-corruption watchdog, fixed parliamentary terms and trials of "deliberative democracy that puts everyday people at the heart of government decision-making."

Asked if he was suggesting politicians were corrupt, Di Natale replied that, without an anti-corruption watchdog, "we don't know the extent of corruption at a federal level."

CLEAN UP POLITICAL DONATIONS

Earlier this week, Liberal Minister Christopher Pyne tip-toed away from the party line by calling for a ban on all non-individual donations —a ban that would curtail the political influence of big money from corporations and third party entities.

This might be the first time such a prominent Liberal Minister has called for reforms to clean up Australia's political donation process.

Cleaning up our democracy will take more than just a ban on corporate and union donations: leaving individual donations unchecked will still allow deep-pocketed individuals to donate huge amounts to political parties, drowning out the voices of ordinary Australians who can't afford to purchase political clout. But Minister Pyne is on the right track: and combining a ban on donations from third parties with a cap on contributions could be just what we need to clean up our political process.

Minister Pyne, alone, won't be loud enough to drown out the powerful vested interests looking to buy influence. Without our support, this might end up as little more than a blip on the radar.

But together, we can show our support for a ban on big donations from big business, and a cap on individual contributions to political parties.

"Clean up political donations," GetUp.

"I make no apologies for saying that big corporate political donations are a very corrosive influence on our democracy," he said, citing lobbying by the hotels and gambling industry against poker machine reform after he entered parliament.

Asked if he would ban union donations, Di Natale said it had long been Greens policy to cap—but implicitly not to ban— donations from individuals and unions, a point that the leader stumbled on in September leading to a correction by the Greens' democracy spokeswoman, Lee Rhiannon.

In an effort to underscore the need for broad political participation, Di Natale invited a young Islamic woman, Nada Kalam, to take the stage and she delivered a short presentation about her experience of racism and concerns about the future including global warming.

Di Natale called for a "people's bank" to improve competition and provide "real help" for first home buyers and people in regional areas.

"Imagine a bank that pursues social objectives like housing affordability, not just profit-driven ones. Which bank? A people's bank."

Di Natale said there was a role for government intervention where market failure existed, including in banking and the energy sector.

He argued that the Western Australian state election, in which Labor, One Nation and the Greens campaigned against asset privatisation, showed people are "sick and tired off flogging off any public asset that isn't nailed down."

"Governments have been punished for [the privatisation] agenda ... So we don't make any apologies for standing with the great majority of Australians who recognise that having a state-owned enterprise might actually deliver things for them, not just for shareholders."

After Di Natale said the Greens would introduce a policy to phase out stamp duty, he was asked whether that would be paid for by broader land taxes or increased council rates.

Di Natale replied that phasing out land tax would need to be "revenue neutral and can't disadvantage people who bought under the existing circumstances". He said the suggested alternative taxes were "a pathway forward" but did not reveal whether they would be the Greens policy.

Di Natale defended his suggestion of a four-day working week and consideration of a universal basic income but refused to give further detail about whether employers or the government would pay for such new entitlements.

The Greens leader said that, given 16% of Australians are underemployed, but about one in four wanted to work less, there was a problem with the distribution of work hours.

"We have an issue when people can't achieve work/life balance and we need legislation to force employers to offer it to them," he said, before adding that some employers offered shorter work weeks already.

Asked how the Greens could achieve political outcomes, Di Natale said it didn't oppose things in the national interest for partisan advantage and had passed legislation with the government including the backpacker tax, Senate voting reform and multinational tax avoidance.

Di Natale took aim at the media, describing it as part of the establishment that was mistrusted by the public and against which Donald Trump had rallied to win popularity.

After a sharp question from the Australian about why the Greens primary vote was behind One Nation and controversy around payment of his au pair, Di Natale joked that News Corp was "the love media."

"When we have got the Australian telling our story for us, it is a challenge ... particularly when it is inaccurate," he said, labelling Fairfax's story about his au pair as "rubbish".

He cited a Press Council ruling that found there was "no reasonable basis" to imply his au pair may have worked up to 40 hours a week.

Di Natale said the Greens found that, when they had "unmediated conversations" with voters, they liked their policies, which made him "confident" the party could achieve his goal of a 20% primary vote within a decade.

> "*Members of Congress were more than three times as likely to meet with individuals when their offices were informed the attendees were donors, an over 200% increase in access.*"

Donors Gain Far Superior Access to Influential Policy Makers

John Wihbey

In the following viewpoint, John Wihbey discusses a 2015 study published by Joshua L. Kalla and David E. Broockman in the American Journal of Political Science called, "Campaign Contributions Facilitate Access to Congressional Officials: A Randomized Field Experiment." This study analyzed data from research gained by a political organization attempting to schedule meetings between its members and high-level officials in nearly 200 congressional offices. The study showed that people were more likely to schedule meetings with high-level officials and senior staff members if they disclosed that they were donors, compared to that of the opposite. Wihbey is an assistant professor of journalism and media innovation at Northeastern University.

As you read, consider the following questions:

1. Why do Joshua L. Kalla and David E. Broockman claim that it is unclear if there is a link between campaign donations and government influence?
2. What percentage of Americans believe that there is too much money in politics?
3. Why does Bob Woodward believe that money in politics is a great story and worth media study?

A *New York Times*/CBS News poll released in June 2015 found a rare point of virtual unanimity among members of the American public: 84% of respondents agreed there is too much money in politics; and a total of 85% said that the current system of campaign finance either needs fundamental reform or should be rebuilt entirely.

The 2012 election cycle saw money flowing from many new sources and the acceleration of *Super PACs* in the context of the new, looser regulatory and legal environment, a result of the Supreme Court's 2010 *Citizens United* decision. According to the Center for Responsive Politics, $6.3 billion was spent during the 2012 election in total—$3.7 billion in Congressional races, and $2.6 billion on the presidential election. The rise of so-called "dark money," a category of financing where the names of backers go undisclosed, makes the effects of all this much harder to trace. Overall, scholars continue to worry that this level of spending by wealthy donors and corporations has the potential to diminish the average citizen's role even further in the democracy.

As money has flooded politics in recent years, news media have certainly pursued some of the consequences and uncovered malfeasance and questionable relationships. However, some longtime observers, such as the *Washington Post*'s Bob Woodward, have noted the need for greater energy and resources for "following the money" at this moment of escalation:

There is a new governing crisis here and it is getting worse. It is about money in politics. It involves both political parties. I won't name names. If you follow the news at all, you know. It is said that the media is sleeping, lost its investigative zeal and does not have the patience to dig. There is some truth to that. But that changes when there is a good story. And money in politics is a great story and important to democracy. It is important that the next president be able, unfettered and unbought, to find and move the country to the next stage of good.

The most palpable and immediate effect of this level of campaign spending on the average voter is a tidal wave of negative political ads, but perhaps the more substantial concern is the long-term effect on the political and legislative process. A 2015 study published in the *American Journal of Political Science*, "Campaign Contributions Facilitate Access to Congressional Officials: A Randomized Field Experiment," analyzed data from a research effort whereby a political organization attempted to schedule meetings between its members and high-level officials in 191 congressional offices. The study's authors—Joshua L. Kalla and David E. Broockman of the University of California at Berkeley—note that, although it may seem obvious that campaign donations might influence governance, the precise connection has remained unclear:

> Evidence that the public, donors, and organized interests believe contributions facilitate access to policy makers has continued to build, yet evidence establishing the causal link between contributions and policy makers' actual behavior has been less forthcoming. Indeed, one of the few points of agreement in the literature on campaign finance is that the available evidence is insufficient for assessing the causal impacts of contributions, both in general ... and with regard to access decisions specifically.

In the study's field experiment, members of the political organization—CREDO Action, a liberal group with 3.5 million members—only sometimes revealed they were campaign donors in order to compare outcomes; to ensure a valid experiment, disclosure of that fact when seeking a meeting was assigned at random.

The study's findings include:

- About half of the congressional offices granted meeting requests overall. However, it helped for the person seeking the meeting to announce he or she was a campaign donor: "Only 2.4% of offices arranged meetings with a member of Congress or chief of staff when they were told the attendees were merely constituents, but 12.5% did so when the attendees were revealed to be donors. In addition, 18.8% of the groups revealed to be donors met with any senior staffer, whereas only 5.5% of the groups described as constituents gained access to a senior staffer, a more than threefold increase."

- Meetings with high-level officials proved much easier when a prior campaign donation was revealed along with a meeting request: "Members of Congress were more than three times as likely to meet with individuals when their offices were informed the attendees were donors, an over 200% increase in access. Putative donors were likewise more than 400% as likely to meet with either a member of Congress or a chief of staff. Strikingly, nearly all the meetings with chiefs of staff and members of Congress occurred in the Revealed Donor condition. When congressional offices were informed only that the attendees were their constituents, attendees very rarely gained access to officials at this level."

"By virtue of having members who had given to political campaigns, the organization in this study was able to obtain far superior access to influential policy makers," the authors conclude. "But not all organizations or individuals can be described as campaign contributors, as many Americans cannot afford to contribute to campaigns. The difference between how congressional offices reacted to the meeting requests when they were and were not aware that organization members had donated thus provides a window into the reception organized groups that contribute to campaigns receive in Washington, shedding light on how they succeed in influencing politics ... and suggesting troubling implications for political equality."

Periodical and Internet Sources Bibliography

The following articles have been selected to supplement the diverse views presented in this chapter.

Zeeshan Aleem, "7 Other Nations That Prove How Absurd U.S. Elections Really Are," Mic.com, May 19, 2015. https://mic.com/articles/118598/7-facts-from-the-around-the-world-show-how-absurd-america-s-elections-really-are#.hMO33QX5P.

Nicole Atwill, "Campaign Finance: Comparative Summary," Library of Congress, May 2009. https://www.loc.gov/law/help/campaign-finance/comparative-summary.php.

Charles W. Bryant, "How Campaign Finance Works," HowStuffWorks.com, November 7, 2017. https://money.howstuffworks.com/campaign-finance7.htm.
"Campaign Contributions Influence Public Policy, Finds Study of 50 State Legislatures," University of Rochester, May 22, 2012. http://www.rochester.edu/news/show.php?id=4060.

Scott Casleton, "It's time for liberals to get over Citizens United," Vox, May 7, 2018. https://www.vox.com/the-big-idea/2018/5/7/17325486/citizens-united-money-politics-dark-money-vouchers-primaries.

Esha Chhabra, "Corporate Social Responsibility: Should It Be A Law?" Forbes, April 18, 2014. https://www.forbes.com/sites/eshachhabra/2014/04/18/corporate-social-responsibility-should-it-be-a-law/#2805d8843736.

David Cole, "How to Reverse Citizens United," The Atlantic, April 2016. https://www.theatlantic.com/magazine/archive/2016/04/how-to-reverse-citizens-united/471504/.

John Craig and David Madland, "How Campaign Contributions and Lobbying Can Lead to Inefficient Economic Policy," Center for American Progress, May 2, 2014. https://www.americanprogress.org/issues/economy/reports/2014/05/02/88917/how-campaign-contributions-and-lobbying-can-lead-to-inefficient-economic-policy/.

Liz Kennedy, "10 Ways Citizens United Endangers Democracy," Demos, January 19, 2012. http://www.demos.org/publication/10-ways-citizens-united-endangers-democracy.

Adam Liptak, "Justices, 5-4, Reject Corporate Spending Limit," NY Times, January 21, 2010. https://www.nytimes.com/2010/01/22/us/politics/22scotus.html.

Stephanie Mencimer, "The Man Behind Citizens United Is Just Getting Started," Mother Jones, May/June 2011. https://www.motherjones.com/politics/2011/05/james-bopp-citizens-united/.

"Support from corporations and labor organizations," Federal Election Commission. https://www.fec.gov/help-candidates-and-committees/candidate-taking-receipts/support-corporations-labor-organizations/

Nick Thompson, "International campaign finance: How do countries compare?" CNN.com, March 5, 2012. https://www.cnn.com/2012/01/24/world/global-campaign-finance/index.html.

CHAPTER 4

Why Is Transparency in Campaign Financing Important to Fair Elections?

Chapter Preface

Transparency in campaign financing is crucial for fair elections, especially in a world that is getting more and more politicized, and a world in which more and more money is funneled into federal election campaigns. It may not be accurate to say that there have been no reforms made to federal campaign finance since the Watergate scandal of the 1970s, but the question is: How successful have those reforms been in making elections fair and transparent today?

Mentioned multiple times throughout this resource, the 2010 *Citizens United* decision has made one of the greatest impacts on federal campaign finance in the modern era, bringing to life further emphasis on the importance of PACs and *Super PACs* and other organizations that are legally allowed to obscure a campaign's donor lists, therefore making it almost impossible for the public to see just how much money is being spent supporting one candidate or one party.

Research conducted by the Pew Research Center reveals the growing concerns on the part of the American people regarding how much influence the massive amounts of money being used to support candidates has on those candidates who are successfully elected to their federal positions. There has been an explosion of funding for federal elections, for example the $1.1 billion spent on the 2014 senate races by candidates, parties and outside groups, which was 25 percent higher than the amount spent in 2010. What sticks out in this metric is that there was an overall drop in voter turnout during the 2014 election cycle, further bringing into light the influence big money has on getting certain candidates elected.

The viewpoints in the following chapter provide deeper insights into the evolution of campaign finance reform in the United States and show just how difficult it still is to enforce any potential violations. The chapter highlights an attempt from the 2016 Bernie Sanders campaign to spotlight perceived violations made by groups supporting his opponent Hillary Clinton's campaign in the Democrat primaries. The manner in which the claims were made shows that it might not be about stopping violations, but rather other unstated reasons that are shown in how the Sanders campaign established its complaint against Clinton's.

"*The IRS has helped facilitate the current system by not investigating whether non-profits are engaged in extensive political activity and abusing tax regulations.*"

After Citizens United the Disconnect Between Average Citizens and Elected Officials Grew

Brennan Center for Justice

*In the following viewpoint, the Brennan Center for Justice describes the difficulties in how the current campaign finance system works in a post-*Citizens United *election circuit. The author's viewpoint induces a list of frequently asked questions regarding campaign donations and the fine line between political spending and political contributions. Additionally, the viewpoint describes the difference between PACs and Super PACs, and how the existence of Super PACs are a direct result of the* Citizens United *ruling from 2010. That ruling claimed that independent political spending, known as spending without coordination with candidates, could not lead to corruption concerns. The Brennan Center for Justice at NYU School of Law is a nonpartisan law and policy institute that works to reform, revitalize, and defend systems of democracy and justice in the United States.*

"Money in Politics 101: What You Need to Know About Campaign Finance After Citizens United," Brennan Center for Justice, September 28, 2012. Reprinted by permission.

As you read, consider the following questions:

1. Can there truly be no corruption concerns regarding independent political spending, as ruled in the 2010 *Citizens United* ruling?
2. Why is consensus difficult in the Federal Election Commission and what can be done to change that?
3. How do corporations get around campaign donation limits, and should this be legal?

Reports on the 2012 election focus as much on the role of big money as they do on the latest polls. One can't read a newspaper without seeing a story on the outsized role of *Super PACs* or the record-breaking amounts spent by secretive non-profits. Hardly an hour passes on the cable news networks without a report on whether Mitt Romney or Barack Obama has more money in the bank.

While there's no shortage of reporting on the latest fundraising totals, it's a lot harder to find any straightforward explanations of how the current campaign finance system works. To help make sense of the current campaign finance system and how it came to resemble the Wild West, here are some answers to frequently asked questions.

Q: There are a lot of stories about unlimited political spending and million dollar donations. Aren't there limits on the size of political contributions?

A: To understand contribution limits, one has to understand that different limits apply depending on who is giving and who is receiving the contributions.

There are limits on donations to candidates and political parties.[1] The Supreme Court has declared that such restrictions are constitutional because allowing unlimited contributions to elected officials (or political parties) could lead to corruption.[2] Current rules set a $2,500 per-person per-election limit for federal candidates.[3] (Each state sets its own limits on donations to state or local candidates.)[4] There is a $30,800 per-person per-year limit on donations to national party committees, and a $10,000 total limit on per-person contributions to state, district or local party committees.[5]

But different rules apply to non-party, outside groups called political action committees, known as PACs. If a PAC contributes directly to candidates, the most a person can donate to the PAC is $5,000.[6] Significantly, if a PAC declares that it will spend its money totally independently from a candidate's campaign, then there are no limits on donations to the PAC. These groups, which can receive unlimited contributions from individuals, corporations, or unions, are commonly called "*Super PACs*."

Finally, some non-profit groups, called "social welfare" organizations, or "501(c)(4) groups," can also accept unlimited contributions from individuals, corporations, and unions. The primary purpose of these groups cannot technically be political, but they can spend substantial amounts on political activities, such as TV commercials.[7]

Q: Is there more outside spending this year than in previous years? How much more?

A: Yes. Outside groups are on pace to spend more during this election than ever before. So far, third party groups—including PACs, *Super PACs*, and 501(c)(4)s—have reported spending nearly $330 million—nearly five times the amount reported at the same point during the 2010 midterm elections and nearly three times the amount reported at the same point during the 2008 elections.[8] With several weeks remaining in the election, the amount of outside spending has surpassed the 2008 total by nearly $30 million, and since outside spending usually spikes in the final month before an election, the total outside expenditures are likely to dramatically increase from four years ago.[9]

Q: About these *Super PACs*—what are they and where did they come from?

A: Traditional PACs wield influence by either donating directly to candidates or spending independently (by airing television advertisements, for example). But traditional PACS have a contribution limit of $5,000 per-person per-year.

By contrast, there are no limits on *Super PAC* donations. *Super PACs* are a consequence of the Supreme Court's ruling in *Citizens United v. FEC*. Remember that the Supreme Court previously upheld donor limits for direct contributions to campaigns and party committees because the Court believed that unlimited contributions could lead to corruption. But in *Citizens United*, the Court declared that independent political spending, because it was not coordinated with candidates, could not lead to corruption concerns.[10]

After *Citizens United*, a federal appellate court in Washington, D.C. heard a case called *SpeechNow.org v. FEC*. In *SpeechNow*, the court interpreted *Citizens United* to mean that as long as a PAC spends its money independently (i.e. does not contribute to, or coordinate with, a candidate), the PAC is free from any contribution limits.[11] Provided a political committee restricts their spending to independent expenditures, it can accept unlimited contributions. These political committees are what is commonly known as *Super PACs*.

Q: So *Citizens United* is responsible for *Super PACs*. Is *Citizens United* responsible for the high levels of outside spending this year?

A: At least in part: the extraordinary levels of outside spending this year would not be possible without *Citizens United*. In the 2010 election, the first campaign cycle after *Citizens United*, outside groups reported spending $298 million, more than a fourfold increase over the amount of outside spending in 2006, the last midterm election before *Citizens United*.[12] Prior to 2010, outside groups engaged in political activity were routinely fined by the FEC for accepting contributions that exceeded federal limits.[13] Seven-figure contributions that undoubtedly would have provoked FEC enforcement actions before 2010 are a major source of *Super PAC* funding today.

As of June 30 2012, 47 donors contributed $1 million or more to *Super PACs*, accounting for 57 percent of individual donations to these groups.[14]

If *Super PACs* had to adhere to the contribution limits in place before *Citizens United*, they would have raised only $11.2 million in contributions from individuals during the 2012 cycle compared to the $346 million they have actually raised. In other words, 97 percent of contributions to *Super PACs* would not have been possible without *Citizens United*.

Q: What about *Super PACs* that work closely with candidates? How can *Super PACs* work closely with campaigns if they're supposed to be "independent?" What are the coordination rules?

A: While *Super PACs* are supposed to be totally independent—after all, that's the only reason they don't have contribution limits—the reality is that they can do a whole lot that looks to most people like "coordination" with campaigns.

The Federal Election Commission sets the rules about what activities are considered independent or "coordinated" with a campaign. At first glance, the rules are simple. As the FEC's website explains, "In general, a payment for a communication is 'coordinated' if it is made in cooperation, consultation or concert with, or at the request or suggestion of, a candidate, a candidate's authorized committee or their agents, or a political party committee or its agents."[15] But the FEC's rules have evolved in such a way that determining what is coordination is now a highly technical and murky exercise.[16]

Unfortunately, the FEC rarely provides clear guidance. Part of the problem is that each party appoints three of the FEC's six commissioners, which makes consensus difficult. A majority vote is required for an advisory opinion. But since *Citizens United*, the Commission has repeatedly deadlocked on specific questions about coordination and independence. When the commissioners split 3-3, the FEC doesn't issue clear guidance.

In perhaps the most notorious case, American Crossroads, Karl Rove's *Super PAC*, requested an opinion from the FEC declaring that advertisements were not "coordinated" with campaigns, even if the candidates appeared in the ads and consulted with the *Super PAC* on developing the scripts. Under any common sense approach, such ads would be deemed coordinated. But not to the FEC—it deadlocked on whether or not such ads constituted "coordinated communications"—and, in the end, the agency offered no guidance at all.[17] In another logic defying ruling, the FEC has said that it is not coordination if a candidate solicits funds for a *Super PAC*.[18]

With no bright line rules about coordination, and with the FEC allowing conduct that would seem to most people to be coordination, *Super PACs* can work extremely closely with campaigns without fear of sanctions.

Q: *Citizens United* also made election spending by corporations legal. How much are corporations spending vs. individuals? What about unions?

A: As of June 30, 2012, businesses had contributed $34.2 million to *Super PACs*, nearly twice the amount donated by unions ($17.3 million). But individuals dominated giving to *Super PACs*, contributing more than $230 million.[19]

But the amount of corporate spending cannot be fully determined because of tax-exempt groups that do not disclose their donors. An investigation by the *New York Times* uncovered several large contributions by corporations to tax-exempt groups, including six- and seven-figure contributions from American Electric Power, Aetna, Prudential Financial, Dow Chemical, Merck, Chevron and MetLife.[20]

By donating to non-profits, corporations can avoid shareholder criticism about using revenues for political purposes as well as consumer reaction to their political stance. Consequently, it is reasonable to suspect that, because of non-profits' ability to hide donations, they are the preferred vehicle for corporate political spending.

Q: Has outside spending benefited one party more than the other?

A: In 2010, conservative groups reported nearly twice the outside spending as liberal groups. So far in the 2012 election cycle, conservative groups have reported three times more spending than liberal groups.[21]

Q: How much outside spending is disclosed vs. not disclosed?

A: During the 2010 election, non-profit "social welfare" organizations—which do not disclose their donors—outspent *Super PACS*—which do—by a 3-2 margin, accounting for $95 million in spending.[22] Trade organizations such as the US Chamber of Commerce, which spent $33 million during the 2010 elections, are also exempt from federal disclosure requirements.[23]

Initial indications suggest that secret spending by non-profits is playing an equally central role in the 2012 elections. The Campaign Media Analysis Group estimates that as of July 2012, dark money totaling nearly $100 million accounted for two-thirds of all spending by the largest outside spenders.[24] *The Huffington Post* found that groups that do not have to disclose their donors had spent $172 million through the end of July—nearly as much as the $174 million spent by outside groups that do disclose their contributors, though total spending by non-profit groups is likely far greater.[25] ProPublica reports that as of July 2012, two of the largest political non-profits, Crossroads GPS and Americans for Prosperity, have eclipsed the combined ad buys of both *Super*

PACs ($55.7 million) and political parties ($22.5 million) with $60 million in television spending.[26]

Non-profit groups have also dramatically escalated spending on express advocacy—ads urging voters to vote for or against specific candidates. Through September 13, 501(c) organizations have spent $67.4 million on express advocacy compared to $44,000 and $3.3 million at the same point in 2006 and 2008 respectively, the two elections before *Citizens United*.[27] Though only a fraction of secret outside spending, the figures offer a snapshot of the growing role of undisclosed spending.

Q: How responsible is the FEC for the current system? What about the IRS?

A: The FEC has helped foster today's hidden system of campaign finance. For example, by not clearly defining what constitutes coordination with a campaign, the FEC has opened the door to all sorts of mischief between campaigns and allegedly independent groups, which, unlike campaigns, do not have donor limits. As a result, contribution limits have been rendered virtually meaningless.

The FEC's failure to enforce federal disclosure laws has also enabled large amounts of secretive spending in elections. Federal law requires groups to report their donors to the FEC if they run either of two types of election advertisements: (a) ads that expressly advocate the election or defeat of candidates (e.g., "Vote for Smith");[28] or (b) "electioneering communications" or "sham issue ads"—ads that mention a specific candidate in the days immediately before an election but stop short of saying "vote for" or "vote against" the candidate (e.g., "Call Smith and tell him to lower taxes").[29] But the FEC has issued regulations that open up giant loopholes in federal disclosure law.[30]

The FEC's regulations say that outside groups only have to report their donors if contributions are earmarked for specific advertisements.[31] Unsurprisingly, almost no donors earmark donations in this way, so the FEC's regulations allow outside spending groups to avoid reporting their donors.

The IRS has helped facilitate the current system by not investigating whether non-profits are engaged in extensive political activity and abusing tax regulations. 501(c)(4) organizations are supposed to be "social welfare" organizations, whose primary purpose is advancing the public good, according to the tax code.[32] Yet these organizations are now operating essentially as unregulated political committees. Like the FEC, the IRS has shirked its regulatory mandate, failing to set unambiguous rules about what percentage of funds these non-profits may spend on political activity. The IRS has an obligation to investigate these groups to ensure they're not violating tax laws. The IRS should revoke tax-exempt status for groups that are political committees in disguise and are primarily engaged in election-related activity, but it has not yet done so.[33]

Q: Are publicly-financed elections the cure for big money in politics? Isn't public financing a failed experiment?

A: After Watergate, Congress adopted a public financing system for presidential elections. The system served the country well for more than two decades. Unfortunately, Congress never modernized the system, and the pool of available public funds did not keep pace with the dramatic escalation in campaign costs. As a result, in 2008, President Obama chose not to use public financing for his primary or general election campaigns. In 2012, neither candidate is using public financing.[34] Reps. David Price (D-NC), Chris Van Hollen (D-MD) and Walter Jones (R-NC) have introduced legislation to repair the presidential campaign finance system.[35] A companion bill has been introduced by Sen. Mark Udall (D-CO).[36]

Public financing has succeeded in several states and cities. Arizona, Connecticut, and Maine, for example, have highly successful public financing systems for state elections. In 2011, the Supreme Court ruled unconstitutional one provision of a certain type of public financing that was used in Arizona that provides additional funding to publicly financed candidates facing high-spending opponents or large amounts of independent expenditures.[37] Nevertheless, the Court reaffirmed the basic constitutionality of public campaign financing.[38]

An alternative, New York City's public financing system, has thrived more than 20 years and is a model for national reform. It poses no constitutional problems. The program is simple, but has powerful consequences. The role of small donors is amplified because donations up to $175 from New York City residents are matched at a rate of 6:1. In other words, a $20 donation is actually worth $140 to the candidate (6 x $20 = $120 + the $20 original contribution = $140). In 2009, small donations and matching funds accounted for 63 percent of the individual contributions in the New York City elections.[39]

Q: What else can be done? What does the future look like?

A: A public financing system based on small donor matching funds can provide an important counterforce to the role of big money. Internet and social media fundraising will make a small donor matching funds system even more powerful. Such a system would decrease the opportunities for corruption of federal officeholders and government decisions. Candidates would have an alternative means to finance their campaigns without becoming obligated to special interests. A small donor matching system should be adopted for both congressional and presidential elections.

But small donor matching funds alone cannot repair the broken campaign finance system. More robust disclosure is necessary so the electorate knows the identities of those seeking to influence them. Congress should pass legislation that replaces the obsolete regulations on "coordination" with meaningful rules that ensure groups claiming to be legally "independent" are not merely campaign subsidiaries. The IRS needs to police groups claiming non-profit status to prevent exclusively political organizations from abusing the tax code by hiding their donors. And the chronically dysfunctional FEC should be replaced by a new agency that does not deadlock along partisan lines, so that the campaign finance laws are actually enforced.

Endnotes

1. See Contribution Limits 2011-2012, FEC, http://www.fec.gov/pages/brochures/contriblimits.shtml (last visited Aug. 12, 2012).

2. Buckley v. Valeo, 424 U.S. 1, 28-29 (1976).

3. Contribution Limits, supra note 1.

4. Nat'l Conference of State Legislatures, State Limits on Contributions to Candidates 2011-2012 (2011), available at http://www.ncsl.org/Portals/1/documents/legismgt/Limits_to_Candidates_2011-2012.pdf.

5. Contribution Limits, supra note 1.

6. Id.

7. Alliance for Justice, Election Year Activities for 501(c)(4) Social Welfare Organizations, available at http://www.afj.org/assets/resources/nap/election-year-activities-for-501c4s.pdf.

8. Ctr. for Responsive Politics, Total Outside Spending by Election Cycle, Excluding Party Committees, OpenSecrets.org, http://www.opensecrets.org/outsidespending/cycle_tots.php?cycle=2012&view=Y&chart=N # viewpt (last visited Sept. 11, 2012).

9. Spending in October of 2010 accounted for more than 57 percent of the outside spending reported during the election cycle. Calculations based on data from the Ctr. for Responsive Politics.

10. Citizens United v. FEC, 130 S. Ct. 876, 910-11 (2010).

11. SpeechNow.org v. FEC, 599 F.3d. 686, 695 (2010).

12. Total Outside Spending, supra note 8.

13. Press Release, Fed. Election Comm'n, FEC to Collect $775,000 Civil Penalty From America Coming Together (Aug. 29, 2007), available at http://www.opensecrets.org/outsidespending/cycle_tots.php?cycle=2012&view=A&chart=N# viewpt; Press Release, Fed. Election Comm'n, FEC Collects $630,000 in Penalties From Three 527 Organizations (Dec. 13, 2006), available at http://www.fec.gov/press/press2006/20061213murs.html; Press Release, Fed. Election Comm'n, Club for Growth Agrees to Pay $350,000 Penalty for Failing to Register as a Political Committee (Sept. 5, 2007), available at http://www.fec.gov/press/press2007/20070905cfg.shtml.

14. Blaire Bowie & Adam Lioz, Demos & U.S. PIRG Educ. Fund, Million-Dollar Megaphones: Super PACs and Unlimited Outside Spending in the 2012 Election 8 (2012), available at http://www.demos.org/sites/default/files/publications/MegaphonesMillionaires-DemosUSPIRG.pdf.

15. Coordinated Communications and Independent Expenditures, FEC (Feb. 2011), http://www.fec.gov/pages/brochures/indexp.shtml#CC.

16. 11 C.F.R. § 109.21.

17. Paul Blumenthal, Karl Rove's 'Fully Coordinated' *Super PAC* Ads Drive the FEC to Deadlock, Huffington Post (Dec. 1, 2012, 3:59 PM), http://www.huffingtonpost. com/2011/12/01/karl-roves-stephen-colbert-fully-coordinated-super-pac-ads_n_1123999.html.

18. Peter H. Stone, Democrats and Republicans Alike Are Exploiting New Fundraising Loophole, iWatchNew.org (July 27, 2011, 5:06 PM), http://www.iwatchnews. org/2011/07/27/5409/democrats-and-republicans-alike-are-exploiting-new-fundraising-loophole.

19. Bowie & Lioz, supra note 14, at 8 fig. 8.

20. Mike McIntire & Nicholas Confessore, Tax-Exempt Groups Shield Political Gifts of Businesses, N.Y. Times, July 7, 2012, at A1.

[21. Ctr. for Responsive Politics, supra note 8.

22. Michael Beckel, Secret Donors Underwrite Attack Ads, iWatchNews.org (June 18, 2012, 3:35 PM), http://www.iwatchnews.org/2012/06/18/9147/nonprofits-outspent-super-pacs-2010-trend-may-continue.

23. McIntire & Confessore, supra note 20.

24. Id.

25. Paul Blumenthal, 'Dark Money' Hits $172 Million in 2012 Election, Half of Independent Group Spending, Huffington Post (July 29, 2012, 6:17 PM), http://www. huffingtonpost.com/2012/07/29/dark-money-2012-election_n_1708127.html.

26. Kim Barker, Two Dark Money Groups Outspending All *Super PACs* Combined, ProPublica (Aug. 12, 2012, 1:50 PM), http://www.propublica.org/article/two-dark-money-groups-outspending-all-super-pacs-combined.

27. Robert Maguire, What Citizens United (et al) Wrought: The Shadow Money Explosion, OpenSecrets Blog (Sept. 18, 2102, 12:53 PM), https://www.opensecrets.org/ news/2012/09/what-citizens-united-et-al-wrought/

28. 2 U.SC. § 434(g)(2).

29. 2 U.S.C. § 434(f).

30. Josh Israel, Court Rules FEC Ignored Law; Shielded Donors from Disclosure, ThinkProgress (Apr. 9, 2012, 4:00 PM), http://thinkprogress.org/ justice/2012/04/09/460378/court-rules-fec-ignored-law-disclosure/

31. 11 C.F.R. § 140.20(c)(9).

32. Social Welfare Organizations, IRS, http://www.irs.gov/Charities-&-Non-Profits/Other-Non-Profits/Social-Welfare-Organizations(last visited Sept. 18, 2012).

33. Press Release, Campaign Legal Ctr., IRS to Consider Changes to 501(c)(4) Eligibility Rules as Requested by Campaign Legal Center and Democracy 21 (July 23, 2012), available at http://www.campaignlegalcenter.org/index.php?option=com_content&view=article&id=1811:july-%2023-2012-irs-to-consider-changes-to-501c4-eligibility-rules-as-requested-by-campaign-legal-center-and-democracy-21&catid=63:legal-center-press-releases&Itemid=61

34. Michael Luo & Jeff Zeleny, Obama, in Shift, Says He'll Reject Public Financing, N.Y. Times, June 20, 2008, at A1.

35. Presidential Funding Act, H. 414, 112th Cong.

36. Presidential Funding Act, S. 3312, 112th Cong.

37. Ariz. Free Enter. Club's Freedom Club PAC v. Bennett, 131 S. Ct. 2806, 2827-2828 (2011).

38. Id., at 2828.

39. Michael J. Malbin, Peter W. Brusoe & Brendan Glavin, 11 Election L.J. 3, 15 (2012).

> "Of the dozen plus laws governing campaign finance that were passed in the last century, the two that define today's system are the creation of the Federal Election Commission (FEC) in 1974 and the McCain-Feingold Act of 2002."

The Rules Surrounding Campaign Finance Are Increasingly Complex

Citizen Joe

In the following viewpoint, the writers at Citizen Joe detail the facts behind campaign finance in the United States since the establishment of the very first law to put in check on how political campaigns could raise money, signed into law in 1867. The viewpoint further details the evolution of the United States' campaign finance regulations, including the Federal Election Campaign Act of 1971, and the amendments in 1974 following the events of the Watergate scandal. What follows was the McCain-Feingold Act, also known as the Bipartisan Campaign Reform Act (BCRA), parts of which were deemed unconstitutional following the 2010 Citizens United ruling. Citizen Joe is a nonpartisan nonprofit organization that aims to engage all Americans in open, fact-based dialogue on national policy debates.

As you read, consider the following questions:

1. What are the differences between hard and soft money?
2. Should candidates have limitations on what money they can spend, depending on how they receive it?
3. Explain the described loopholes around soft money spending on campaign contributions and how those loopholes can be closed.

You probably couldn't tell from the 2004 election, but in 2002 Congress set strict limits on how much money can go into federal campaigns. The McCain-Feingold Act, as it's commonly known, was passed with the intent of closing loopholes in earlier campaign finance laws. Opponents of the reform are troubled by how it limits the 1st Amendment right to free association and free speech. Cynics suspect that no matter how much you regulate campaign spending, people with political opinions and money to burn will find a way to toss their 2-plus cents into the election fray; 527's are the latest example.

The Laws

In 1867 Congress passed the first law putting a check on how political campaigns could raise money (by saying government employees couldn't wedge money out of naval yardworkers). Campaign finance laws have been expanding—and getting more complicated—ever since.

Of the dozen plus laws governing campaign finance that were passed in the last century, the two that define today's system are the creation of the Federal Election Commission (FEC) in 1974 and the McCain-Feingold Act of 2002. (OpenSecrets)

Federal Election Campaign Act (1971) and its Amendments (1974)

The Federal Election Campaign Act (FECA) and its harder hitting 1974 amendments took the hodge-podge of earlier finance laws and wrapped them into a neat comprehensive package, limiting how much federal campaigns could spend and how much individuals could give to political committees, parties and candidates. Perhaps most importantly, the '74 amendments set up the Federal Election Commission (FEC) to oversee that campaigns were following the rules.

McCain-Feingold Act - aka BRCA (FEC)

The McCain-Feingold Act of 2002, officially the Bipartisan Campaign Reform Act (BCRA), set the campaign finance rules we have today. Its main shift was to abolish "soft money"—unlimited money that could be used toward "party building" activities. BCRA also set limits on "issue ads," which were seen as a loophole to the finance laws. The chart below compares the regulations of the FECA era compared to the BCRA.

Explainer: Hard and Soft Money

The trouble with defining these terms is that they mean different things to different people in different contexts. Clear? Here's the deal: before BCRA, soft and hard money were clearly defined. Hard Money was any regulated money—that is, money that is capped - that could be given to support a specific candidate or campaign (example: giving money to the Bush '00 campaign). Soft Money was unregulated money—with no limits on how much could be given – that could go to a political party for 'party building' purposes and grass roots efforts but could not go towards a candidate's campaign (example: money to register voters, hand out party bumper stickers). How the terms are used today : Although soft money technically doesn't exist—and so all money given to parties and candidates is regulated "hard" money, people still use both terms to describe "hard" and "soft" money that swills around outside candidate and party coffers (the most common example are the 527s, which are not regulated by the FEC). Some also loosely use "soft money" to describe funds used for the old soft money party building purposes, although, again, technically since parties can only collect is regulated "hard" money, all money that parties spend is "hard money."

The BRCA rules
Who Can Give

- Individuals. See the chart below on how much.
- Political Committees. Political committees and all their variants—political action committees, or PACs, and leadership PACs—are independent groups that come together to help elect candidates. They raise money that they can then hand over to party committees and candidates. Like individuals, they're limited in how much they can give (from $5000 - $26,700). PAC contributions are a drop in the bucket for the presidential races, but pay for roughly a third of congressional races (OS).
- Party Committees. These are political committees that officially represent a local or national party. They have limits in how much they can give candidates, but they can transfer funds between other party committees to their hearts' desire.

HOW MUCH INDIVIDUALS CAN GIVE	PRE-BCRA	TODAY
To any candidate (per election)	$1,000	$2,300
To any national party committee (per year)	$20,000	$28,500
To any PAC, state or local party committee (per year)	$5,000	$10,000
Total that an individual can give	$25,000 (per year)	$108,200 (per two year cycle)

Note: numbers are adjusted each year for inflation. Also see the FEC's chart for more details on how much committees, PACs, etc. can give.

Hybrid PACs and 527s

In addition to "super PACs" (which can raise and spend unlimited funds) and regular political action committees (which raise money via contributions capped at $5,000 per election), there are several other vehicles donors can use to attempt to influence elections. These include Carey committees (also known as hybrid PACs), which maintain one account for making contributions to candidates, like regular PACs, and a separate account for making independent expenditures, like super PACs. In addition, there are "527 organizations" and 501(c) nonprofit groups. The 527s can be entirely political and must disclose their donors. However, 501(c)(4) groups can shield their donors' identities—but, under IRS rules, can't have politics as their primary purpose.

"2018 Outside Spending, by Group," The Center for Responsive Politics.

Who Can't Give

Corporations and unions cannot give money to candidates or committees, although they can spend money on other organizing efforts (see loopholes below). Foreigners who are not citizens or legal residents and government contractors also cannot give to federal campaigns.

Who Can Receive—and What They Can Spend Their Money On

- Political committees can receive limited donations from individuals and other committees and, as mentioned above, can give limited amounts to candidates. They can spend unlimited funds, however, on "independent expenditures."
- Party committees can receive limited money from individuals and other committees and unlimited money from other party committees. They can give a limited amount to candidates and can spend limited funds on "coordinated"

expenditures, but can spend an unlimited amount on "independent expenditures."

- Candidates can receive limited amounts from individuals and committees, but once they get their money, they can spend it where they please.

Softish Money That's Still Around (aka Loopholes)

In spite of the strict rules limiting money to committees and candidates, campaign finance rules allow some softish money in to the committee world (for example, Levin funds), while it leaves other spenders of election related money completely off the hook (for example, individuals).

- Independent expenditures. Individuals, groups of individuals and committees can spend an unlimited amount of money promoting a candidate—as long as they don't coordinate with the candidate or her party. If you're a group and you raise more than $1000, however, you'd have to register as a committee, and so be limited in how much money you could raise from individuals. But if you're a gazillionaire and you operate on your own, you can spend as many of your gazillions as you'd like on ads supporting or attacking a candidate. (FEC)
- Levin funds. Individuals (and corporations and unions, if state law says it's okay) can give up to $10,000 on top of the limits listed above to local and state parties for grassroot get-out-the-vote type activities. (FEC)
- Corporations and unions are free to spend unlimited money on:
  - Voter registration and get-out-the-vote activities directed at their stockholders, employees and members.
  - Setting up and running a political action committee (for the committee's overhead costs).
- Millionaires and the millionaire's amendment. Candidates with a lot of cash of their own are free to spend as much

as they'd like to support their campaign. As part of BRCA, candidates running against the mega rich (or those who spent more than $350,000 of their own money for a House race), had more lenient limits on how much they could raise for their counter campaign. The Supreme Court, however, ruled that "millionaire's amendment" illegal in June '08. (*WP*)

- Conventions. Convention hosting committees and the money they raise to run the Democratic and Republican conventions are not regulated by campaign finance rules.

- Issue ads. Before BRCA, corporations and unions had no restrictions on their ability to pay for "issue ads"—ads that supposedly only express an opinion on an issue but everyone knows are supporting or opposing one candidate. Now these ads can't be shown 30 days before a primary or 60 days before a general election—but outside those time limits, they're still free to air. Now, however, the Supreme Court have given "grass-roots" groups a loophole to air ads that target candidates before elections, provided the ad is not about the election (*WP*), saying BRCA went too far when it limited groups' ability to mention candidates' names in issue ads (the FEC will try to make sense of that ruling in regulations by December '07—*WP*). Another court, meanwhile, says the FEC doesn't go far enough in restricting how much groups and individuals can coordinate with campaigns in whipping out independent ads (*WP*).

- Ballot measure issue ads. The FEC voted in August 2005 to allow unlimited soft money to go toward issue ads supporting or opposing state ballot initiatives.

- Movies and movie ads. 2004 gave birth to the election flic—with films like *Fahrenheit 911* drawing a thin line between art and electioneering. But, along with books and news media, films are not currently regulated—and because of their special protections under the first amendment, it's doubtful that will change soon—but the FEC was considering changes in late 2005.

- 501(c)s. Some of these nonprofits are allowed to spend money on get-out-the-vote activities and issue advocacy. Although campaign finance law loosely regulates 501(c)s, these organizations have to comply with IRS rules which also limit how they can spend their money. The FEC was considering regs for 501(c)3s in late 2005.
- The press and, as of March 2006 (*WP*), internet sites are exempt from campaign finance rules (excepting, of course, for paid political advertising).
- And then there are 527s...

See the Federal Elections Commission for a pretty thorough backgrounder on McCain-Feingold.

527's

527's, named after the IRS code they fall under, are tax-exempt organizations that engage in political activities. They became big players during the 2004 Presidential election because they are NOT covered by the BCRA, and so could take in unlimited money contributions.

The Loophole

- Though 527's cannot endorse a candidate, receive party funding, or collaborate with a candidate's campaign, there are no restrictions on opposing a candidate as long as they're acting as free agents
- Since they are not bound by the BCRA, they can advertise throughout the 60 days prior to the election, including election day

Spending
Of the 471 registered 527's

- 2004–$554 million
  - Democratic or liberal organizations—$365 million (OS)

- Republican or conservative organizations—$140 million (OS)
- 2000—$149 million

For a list of the largest 527's, see PublicIntegrity.org. To see the 527 code itself, see Cornell's Legal Information Institute (https://www.law.cornell.edu/wex).

Past and Current Spending—The Big Picture

We tried to bring together all the fundraising numbers from the past few presidential cyles to give the full picture of all the money that goes into federal elections. We got pretty close. For what's

	2004	2000	1996
Presidential Campaigns (including primaries, general elections and federal funding)	$718 - $731 million	$343 million	$240 million
Republican and Democratic Parties (national and local)*	$1.6 billion	$1.2 billion	-
House candidates	$696 million	$572 million	$478 million
Senate candidates	$490 million	$435 million	$287 million
527s	$554 million	$149 million	-
Convention Committees	$138 million	$56 million	-

missing—beside the empty boxes—see "loopholes" above. All the numbers are drawn from PoliticalMoneyLine, the US Census, OpenSecrets, Public Integrity, and the Campaign Finance Institute.

*2000 data includes soft money contributions

Public Funding

Since 1976, presidential nominees have had the option of requesting federal funding for their campaigns. The catch is, if they accept federal cash, they have to also agree to limit their campaign spending to the amount of funds they get and not accept more contributions. In 2004, both Bush and Kerry passed on federal funds—which amounted to $75 million apiece. For more on federal funding, see the FEC's surprisingly clear guide. The *Washington Post* doesn't see candidates going for public funding in '08 either (*WP*).

Where The Facts Are From:

FEC—Federal Election Commission—government site

OpenSecrets—site of The Center for Responsive Politics, a non-profit research group that tracks money in politics

WP—Washington Post—mainstream newsapaper

*"The increase in campaign money
spent resulted in a record $24 spent
on each Senate vote cast in 2014,
compared with about half that
amount in the previous off-year cycle
of 2010."*

As More Money Flows into Campaigns, Americans Worry About Its Influence

Drew Desilver and Patrick van Kessel

*In the following viewpoint, Drew Desilver and Patrick van Kessel
argue that despite the curent partisan environment, people from
all parties tend to agree that campaign spending is almost out of
control and the high cost of campaigning is discouraging many quality
candidates from partaking in a costly election like that for president.
Furthermore, the viewpoint shows how much money has been spent
in recent elections, including the 2012 presidential election cycle,
which was more than $1.4 billion, and the $24 spent on each Senate
vote cast in 2014, totaling $1.1 billion. DeSilver is a senior writer
at Pew Research Center. Van Kessel is a senior data scientist at Pew
Research Center.*

As you read, consider the following questions:

1. Per the viewpoint, which election was the costliest since the modern disclosure rules kicked in? Why was it so costly?
2. Why is there no correlation between election spending and voter turnout?
3. How much money have *Super PACs* spent since 2010?

Americans of different political persuasions may not agree on much, but one thing they do agree on is that money has a greater—and mostly negative—influence on politics than ever before. Among liberals and conservatives, Republicans and Democrats, large majorities favor limits on campaign spending and say the high cost of campaigning discourages many good candidates from running for president.

While perceptions of influence are subjective, there's clearly more money in the US political system now than at any time since the campaign finance reforms of the 1970s, according to a new Pew Research Center data analysis of contributions and spending. That's the case whether you look at presidential, House or Senate elections.

Last year's midterm Senate election was the costliest ever—or at least since 1974, when modern disclosure rules kicked in. The 2014 election featured several competitive races, the outcomes of which would determine control of the Senate; Democrats and Republicans fought—and spent—fiercely. According to our analysis of Campaign Finance Institute data, nearly $1.1 billion was spent on 2014's Senate races by candidates, parties and outside groups, 25% more than in the previous off-year cycle of 2010. The biggest increase was in non-party independent expenditures, which soared from $105.6 million (inflation-adjusted) to $387.3 million.

But despite all that money and attention, voter turnout in last year's Senate elections didn't increase; in fact, it was the lowest since 1990. We calculated turnout using estimates of the voting-eligible population (all citizens of voting age, at home and abroad, excepting ineligible felons) made by University of Florida political scientist Michael McDonald. Only about 44 million people voted for Senate in 2014, according to tabulations published by the House Clerk's office—38% of the voting-eligible population in those states with Senate elections.

Across the Rotunda, $1.1 billion was spent last cycle on House elections by candidates, parties and outside groups, according to our analysis of the CFI data. That was somewhat less than in the 2010 and 2012 election cycles (after adjusting for inflation), but still a substantial amount, given that only a few dozen House races were considered competitive going in. Nearly 79 million people voted in House races last year, or 35% of the estimated voting-eligible population—the lowest turnout level since 1998.

The increase in campaign money spent, combined with the drop in actual turnout, resulted in a record $24 spent on each Senate vote cast in 2014, compared with about half that amount—$12.74—spent in the previous off-year cycle of 2010, our analysis found. Spending per House vote cast wasn't quite a record in 2014: $14.05 per vote, a similar level to the previous two midterms. (Per-vote spending on House races tends to drop significantly in presidential-election years.)

In presidential races, we examined in detail Federal Election Commission data on contributions and expenditures from 2000 to the present. Total receipts, the total amount of reported cash that flows into a campaign from outside sources, peaked in the 2008 election cycle, at more than $1.8 billion ($2.03 billion in inflation-adjusted dollars)—nearly triple the receipts of such committees in 2000.

In the 2012 cycle, only the Republicans had an active primary season, but that didn't stop the flow of political money: Official campaigns still had total receipts of nearly $1.4 billion ($1.44 billion in constant dollars), according to our analysis.

It's still early in the 2016 presidential cycle, with the first-in-the-nation Iowa caucuses two months away. But the two dozen

Demands for FEC Reform

In the Issue Brief, "The FEC: The Failure to Enforce Commission," Wertheimer and Simon explain how the Federal Election Commission has thwarted campaign finance regulations and now consistently stymies efforts to enforce campaign finance regulations laws intended to provide transparency of how our campaigns are financed and curb corruption of elections and government decisions.

Structural impediments of the six-member FEC and its inability "to take significant enforcement actions on its own" have helped to create a "completely dysfunctional" agency. "We have reached the point," the authors write, "where we have the illusion of campaign laws because in reality, there is little or no enforcement of these laws."

One of the FEC's most detrimental attributes is its political makeup. The authors note that House and Senate leaders have influenced the shape of the FEC by sending names to the president who "routinely forwards them to the Senate for confirmation," thereby undercutting the Supreme Court's decision in *Buckley v. Valeo*, which found the appointment process of the Commission that allowed congressional leaders to appoint members is unconstitutional.

Today, the FEC's inability to enforce campaign finance laws can be traced to its "three Republican commissioners" who are "ideologically opposed to the campaign finance laws."

The authors continue, "The Republican commissioners have consistently blocked the agency's professional staff from pursuing enforcement matters, and have worked to prevent laws on the books from being properly interpreted. This concerted campaign has effectively shut down any significant enforcement of the nation's campaign finance laws, and has made the FEC nonfunctional." (The authors provide numerous examples of the Republican commissioners' efforts to scuttle enforcement efforts regarding possible campaign finance violations by both Democratic and Republican groups.)

Wertheimer and Simon argue that the FEC must be reformed, but not with incremental steps.

"Democracy 21/ACS Issue Brief: A New Federal Agency is Needed to Enforce Campaign Finance Laws," Democracy 21, February 21, 2013.

or so official presidential campaign committees collectively have raised more than $278 million, according to our analysis. Among Democrats, Hillary Clinton ($77.5 million) is leading Bernie Sanders ($41.5 million) and Martin O'Malley ($3.3 million), while Ben Carson ($31.4 million), Ted Cruz ($26.6 million) and Jeb Bush ($24.8 million) are pacing the crowded GOP field.

But the official campaign structures aren't the whole story. Independent expenditures, so called because they are supposed to be uncoordinated with the official campaigns, have become increasingly prominent in recent years. (Note: None of our analyses include so-called 527 organizations, tax-exempt groups that engage in political activities and report to the IRS rather than the Federal Election Commission. Federal contribution and spending rules don't apply to 527s, so long as they don't expressly advocate for a candidate's election or defeat. While prominent for several years in the mid-2000s, their role has largely been taken over by "*Super PACs*," discussed below.)

Independent expenditures can expressly advocate for a candidate's election or defeat. They can be made both by political party committees and by outside groups so long as they are not made in direct coordination with a candidate. These include so-called *Super PACs* that became possible after two 2010 court rulings, *Citizens United v. FEC* and *SpeechNow.org v. FEC*. After the 2002 McCain-Feingold law banned political parties from raising or spending "soft money" on elections, the parties greatly increased their independent expenditures—to $265 million in 2004, from $5.7 million in 2002.

Super PACS can raise unlimited funds from individuals, corporations and unions, and spend the money to directly advocate for or against candidates, so long as their activities aren't coordinated with an official campaign or party. Since they became legal, *Super PACs* have rapidly become a major force in US politics. Collectively, according to our analysis, they made independent expenditures of $65 million in 2010, $608 million in the 2012 presidential election cycle and $339 million in the 2014 mid-term election cycle.

So far in the current cycle, according to the Center for Responsive Politics, 1,260 *Super PACs* have raised a total of $313.5 million and spent $73.2 million. Most of the major presidential candidates have at least one *Super PAC* supporting them; the one backing Jeb Bush, Right to Rise USA, had nearly $98 million on hand as of June 30, its most recent reporting date.

> *"Is this a fact-check? No. There's a shortage of facts here, since we can't see the books of the various committees."*

It Is Difficult to Determine When Joint Fundraising Committees Violate Campaign Laws

Peter Overby

In the following viewpoint, Peter Overby details claims made by Bernie Sanders' election campaign against the Hillary Clinton Victory Fund, and that the organization "seriously violated" the United States' campaign finance laws. Overby goes into detail how a campaign like Clinton's can accept a significant donation from someone like actor George Clooney and still be within the legal limits set forth in the United States' campaign rulings, and then explains the Sanders Campaign's claims that the joint committee is subsidizing the Clinton Campaign in staff salaries and overhead. Much of the viewpoint also shows that, due to current laws, it is very difficult to determine if the Clinton Campaign and the Hillary Victory Fund have, in fact, violated campaign law. Overby reports on campaign finance and lobbying for NPR.

"Clinton Fundraising Violations? A Breakdown Of Sanders' Claims," by Peter Overby, NPR, April 19, 2016. Reprinted by permission.

As you read, consider the following questions:

1. What is a joint fundraising committee and is it the same or different from a PAC or *Super PAC*?
2. How are campaign contributions allocated so that a candidate stays within the United States' campaign finance regulations?
3. Why did the Sanders campaign decide to take its accusations to the DNC, not the Federal Election Commission?

Bernie Sanders' campaign is accusing the Hillary Victory Fund of "serious apparent violations" of the campaign finance law. The Hillary Victory Fund is a joint fundraising committee for the Clinton campaign, the Democratic National Committee and 32 state Democratic Party committees.

Is this a fact-check? No. There's a shortage of facts here, since we can't see the books of the various committees. This appears to be a political attack more than a legal case.

First, a word about joint fundraising committees. They're alliances of candidates and party political committees (or groups of candidates) to raise money together. A donor writes one check to the joint fundraising committee and the funds are divided up, according to the contribution limits. They're a regular part of presidential campaigning.

Joint committees operate alongside the campaign and party committees, usually focusing on major donors. For the Hillary Victory Fund, the first $2,700 goes to Clinton's campaign, the next $33,400 to the DNC, and the rest in $10,000 bites to state committees. Events such as George Clooney's $353,400 fundraiser last weekend are where these checks are collected.

What's the point of a presidential joint fundraising committee? To raise big-donor money beyond the reach of the campaign and to amass funds and build infrastructure for the general election contest. So far the Hillary Victory Fund has raised $60 million.

Significantly, it is building its cash on hand to use down the road; that amount was $15.9 million on March 31.

Moving on to the specifics.

The claim: Hillary Victory Fund is raising some money exclusively for the Clinton campaign, not for the party committees.

In a letter to DNC Chairwoman Debbie Wasserman Schultz, Sanders campaign lawyer Brad Deutsch says the Hillary Victory Fund has done small-donor fundraising that only benefits Clinton.

The short answer: Joint fundraising committees can do that along with their big-donor fundraising.

The long answer: In 2015, the Hillary Victory Fund raised $5.2 million in contributions of $2,700 or less. It also raised $20.1 million from donors who gave between $3,000 and $366,400 each. (Receipts jumped this year, but deeper data aren't yet available.)

Beyond that, details are thin. The letter cites the Hillary Victory Fund's spending on direct-mail and online fundraising, "both of which appear to benefit only [the Clinton campaign]" because of the $2,700 contribution limit. But while mail and online pitches are aimed at small donors, they don't rule out people giving more than that. Clinton aides say the allegation is false; there are no data to contradict them. It's unknowable with the current Federal Election Commission disclosures alone.

The claim: The letter says there are "serious concerns" that the joint committee is subsidizing the Clinton campaign in staff salaries and overhead.

The short answer: We can't tell.

The long answer: Somebody has to run the joint committee. Here, it's the Clinton campaign. The Sanders campaign points to $2.6 million in payments from the joint committee to the campaign, labeled as "salaries and overhead expenses." But there's no way of knowing exactly whose salaries and which overhead that's paying for.

The letter is two pages, with assertions and broad totals, but no citations of specific transactions. From all visible records, the Hillary Victory Fund seems to be operating much like other joint committees.

Again, this is a matter of politics, not law. If it were a legal complaint, the Sanders campaign would have gone to the Federal Election Commission, not the DNC. Then again, the FEC would deal with the complaint slowly, if at all.

The small irony here is that Sanders has a joint fundraising committee too: Bernie Victory Fund. The DNC set it up for him last year when it established the Hillary Victory Fund. But the Bernie Victory Fund has remained dormant and Sanders has relied on his base of small donors instead.

And just minutes after sending out the complaint to the DNC, the Sanders campaign sent out a fundraising letter to supporters citing the Clinton joint fundraising committee as a reason to give to Sanders.

> "*A recent poll showed that 82% of Americans believe congressional candidates should be banned from receiving contributions from industries 'vital to the financial and national security of the country.'*"

Campaign Finance Reform Restructured Campaigns and the Political World

Laura MacCleery

In the following viewpoint, an excerpt from Laura MacCleery's paper from the Catholic University of America's Columbus School of Law, MacCleery describes the reforms made to the United States' campaign finance laws during the early 2000s and how the McCain-Feingold Act, also known as The Bipartisan Campaign Reform Act of 2002, impacted the 2008 election cycle. The viewpoint goes on to show the impact of high-level donors has been significant in politics even before the recent campaign reforms, and the cap on contributions from high-level donors has encouraged a shift to donating not to specific candidates, but to the parties themselves. MacCleery is the former Deputy Director of the Campaign Finance program for the Brennan Center for Justice and an experienced consumer advocate.

As you read, consider the following questions:

1. Per the viewpoint, what was unique about the 2008 election cycle and how did the BCRA emphasize that?
2. How much money did the DNC find was donated by only 168 people during the 1996 election cycle?
3. What is better, allowing donors to donate as much as they want to a specific candidate or to a specific political party? Detail your reasoning.

O n the heels of the 2008 election, a crucial question for campaign finance reformers is whether the much-heralded small-donor revolution represents a meaningful and lasting change in the composition of political donors in the electorate.

Of course, an open-seat contest for the presidency is unusual in the span of history, and the successful campaign by President Obama is both a testament to the candidate and to the shift in political winds that made the nation receptive to political change. Indeed, Obama's candidacy was ground-breaking in many ways, not the least of which was the manner in which his campaign made use of lightning-fast, low-cost, Internet-based technologies both for organizing supporters and for gathering contributions.

Although it is possible that such a campaign could have taken shape in this way without a change in the campaign finance landscape, it is equally true that a set of key reforms in campaign financing—in particular the passage of the 2002 Bipartisan Campaign Reform Act (BCRA)—laid the groundwork for it, altering incentives that had, prior to the 2008 election cycle, helped push the political parties out of the arms of large, corporate donors and into doing the important work of recruiting contributions from individuals.

[...]

Law matters, and future changes that would water down or overturn these rules would mean a significant step backward.

This shift has been dramatic and has occurred over a scant few election cycles at an accelerating pace. The landmark reforms of BCRA (also widely known as "McCain-Feingold" for its Senate co-sponsors) were preceded by several decades of political neglect of all but the largest individual donors. Due to a number of factors, including a political realignment of the electorate indicated by the appeal of Reagan-era Republicanism,[2] the Democratic Party moved away from its base starting in the 1980s, and increasingly toward the political center. The shift helped the Democratic Party compete with Republicans for wealthy donors and corporate dollars, but it also led to—and reinforced—a growing addiction to unregulated, so-called "soft money."

[...]

Instead, over the past year, experts across the political spectrum have pointed to the alleged "collapse of the campaign finance regime."[4] While the campaign finance playing field experienced a marked shift after BCRA, this shift was far from a collapse.

[...]

Some of these transformations were likely beyond the purview of reformers who advocated for BCRA because of the abuses of power and scandals in the 1990s. To the extent BCRA was motivated by a backwards-looking view, it was a limited reform aimed at the biggest single abuse in the system and was intended to restore some of the integrity of the existing campaign finance restrictions, which had badly eroded over time.[5] It was never, as critics often mistakenly suggest,[6] intended to reduce the amount of money in politics or to solve all of the problems plaguing the system, and it certainly has not done so.

Nonetheless, the case for BCRA was also forward-looking, and it has been a resounding success in meeting those objectives. The hope and clear intent of reformers was that eliminating the nearly limitless amounts of "soft money" would democratize fundraising in just the manner that did in fact happen.[7] In so doing, the soft-money restrictions did, as the section heading in the law provided, effect a "reduction of special interest influence."[8]

Consider a single fact: when the Democratic National Committee (DNC) conducted an internal study to determine the sources of its funds in 1997, it found that a very small number of wealthy contributors were responsible for a shockingly high percentage of overall soft-money contributions.[9] Nearly $25 million—or twenty percent of the total $122 million collected in 1996—had been contributed by just 168 people.[10]

BCRA changed this distribution curve dramatically. As Thomas E. Mann, a Senior Fellow in Governance Studies at the Brookings Institution, observed about the presidential primary elections in July 2008:

> Large soft-money contributions to parties from corporations, unions, and wealthy individuals (often arranged through intense pressure from elected and party officials) are no longer a part of the picture. Presidential candidates have focused on hard-money contributors, which are limited to $2,300 per donor.[11]

[...]

BCRA had a positive impact on parties in two significant ways: First, the law provided a cap on contributions to candidates that encouraged high donors to give more money directly to the parties; and second, it pushed the parties toward individual contributions by eliminating soft money. As David Magleby noted in his comprehensive new book, *The Change Election: Money, Mobilization, and Persuasion in the 2008 Federal Elections*:

> BCRA encouraged the parties to raise money from individuals by increasing the aggregate contribution limits for individuals wishing to contribute to parties and by indexing these contributions to inflation. ... By banning the unlimited soft money contributions from individuals and groups and especially from unions and corporate general funds, BCRA added another reason for parties to emphasize raising money from individuals.[12]

Importantly, none of the vocal concerns about the potential negative consequences of BCRA, including the myriad predictions of profound harm to the Democratic party,[13] have come true. In the run-up to its passage, the conventional wisdom held that Democratic candidates would be bereft of the soft-money donations they would need to compete with Republicans' traditional donor base.[14]

In fact, BCRA has not been the political parties' "suicide pact;" instead, the parties are flourishing under it.[15] In the two elections prior to the enactment of BCRA, the national parties raised over $2 billion, almost half of which was unregulated soft money. In the 2004 and 2006 elections—the first two after BCRA went into effect—the parties raised more so-called "hard money," or contributions from individuals subject to BCRA's federal contribution limits, than they did in the two previous elections.[16] As David Magleby noted, "the Republican National Committee and the Democratic National Committee raised more hard money alone in 2004 than they had in both soft and hard money contributions combined in 2002."[17]

More recent data from the Federal Election Commission shows that in the 2008 election, the parties' national fund-raising committees "overshadowed" pre-BCRA totals by $149.8 million ($129 million for Democrats and $21 million for Republicans) in comparison with the 2000 election, and by $249 million ($191 million for Democrats and $58 million for Republicans) in comparison with the 2002 election.[18]

While the amount of money has increased, the collateral consequences of raising money in a different way have been astonishing. BCRA's ban, by cutting off the flow of unregulated money into party coffers, pushed the national parties to reach out aggressively to both new and smaller donors, reconnecting the parties to a broad base of individual donors who are both its financial and ideological enthusiasts.

[...]

Additionally, having learned from Democratic primary candidate Howard Dean about the burgeoning potential of the Internet for soliciting donations and organizing, both presidential candidates in the 2004 election raised unprecedented amounts of money in small contributions.

In 2008, those lessons were most fully applied in the presidential race by the Obama campaign, which sought to harness the power of the Internet outreach to small donors as a source of legitimacy and independence. While the party infrastructure played a role in the general election, it was overshadowed by Obama's strategy for full-circle organizing, which required a central appeal, candidate-led coordination, and broad base of mobilized supporters. BCRA pushed the parties to transform themselves, and the political candidates, particularly the presidential candidates, absorbed these lessons well.

As Brian Wolff, Chair of the Democratic Congressional Campaign Committee (DCCC), recently summarized to The American Prospect, BCRA "forced us to do what we should have been doing all along, which was including more people in the political process."[20] This approach to political fund-raising stands in stark contrast to the Democrats' pre-BCRA strategy in which, according to Wolff, "[Democrats] basically reached out to labor unions and said, give to this member of Congress. ... Nothing was programmatic."[21]

By forcing parties to invest in the harder challenge of appealing to a larger number of individual donors rather than a small cadre of wealthy donors, BCRA increased public engagement by the parties. Coupled with transformational changes in campaign practices made possible by the Internet, this new focus enhances the legitimacy of those elected by engaging many more people in the process.

When the new limits on large contributions became meaningful, the reforms created a space for smaller donations to matter and enabled more individuals to reconnect to the parties and candidates. When coupled with the new Internet-based tools and an emphasis on community organizing principles, the changes have been profound, extending far beyond fundraising to include a renewed spirit of volunteerism, increased online and offline activism, and party structures that are becoming more bottom-up and far less top-down.[22] The parties' attitudinal shift toward their members and activists is a little-chronicled but highly-welcomed development, and was, in fact, linked to the changes spurred by BCRA as it weaned the parties off of their dependency on large contributions and donors.

These salutary changes point the way to future reforms that would further enhance political engagement, including rewarding political investments in small donors by using matching funds and public funding systems. Moreover, subsequent elections will likely see far more candidates in congressional and state-level elections who will likely benefit from the newly revitalized party infrastructures and their deeper connections to individuals.

[…]

Conclusion: A Time for Action to Improve Democracy

Today is clearly a pivotal point in American political life. High voter turnout and grassroots fund-raising revitalized the 2008 election; but big promises in the face of extraordinary challenges leave the President and Congress vulnerable to an expectation gap. Younger voters—particularly those of the so-called "millennial generation"—will want to see results, and inaction risks their disenchantment and frustration.[345]

It will be devastating if those with a professed faith in democracy do not live up to campaign promises of competence, transparency, and change. Measures that enhance public faith in Congress's ability to conduct meaningful oversight are essential, but asking for real change from members who must continue to raise money from regulated industries will be difficult, if not impossible. In light of the need to address looming crises in health care, energy, and finance, a better source of campaign funding is needed.

Democratic institutions are the public commons, but they have been privatized to our detriment. A recent poll showed that eighty-two percent of Americans believe congressional candidates should be banned from receiving contributions from industries "vital to the financial and national security of the country."[346] Meanwhile, another poll showed that seventy-three percent of voters believe that political donations to lawmakers were "a major factor in causing the current financial crisis on Wall Street," and more than two-thirds of voters support public funding of congressional elections.[347]

However, public opinion does not generally track the state of the law in this area. Forty-two percent of Republicans thought that participation in the presidential public funding system should be mandatory (although public funding systems must be voluntary to be constitutional under prevailing law), and fifty-seven percent of all Americans favored spending limits, which are also unconstitutional. The intense public support for spending limits, even for mandatory public financing, is evidence of the deep skepticism that the public harbors about the role of money in politics.[348]

A system of public financing would also lift up the grassroots. More than two-thirds of the 500,000 Obama volunteers that answered the campaign's post-election survey responded that they "would like to continue to volunteer in the communities as part of an Obama for America 2.0 organization."[349] By providing this burgeoning small-donor movement with a next-stage role, a revitalized campaign finance structure would help ensure that progressive ideas encounter a political structure that can support them.[350]

Public funding would enable members of Congress to listen to, and trust in the support of, their constituents. They would also spend less time fund- raising, and more time solving the critical challenges of the day. According to a study in American Politics Research, candidates who participate in full public funding programs spent sixty-six percent less time doing fundraising.[351] The study also found that candidates who participated in public funding spent just eight percent of their personal schedules on fundraising, as compared with twenty-four percent for other major party candidates.[352]

Moreover, even with all of the positive developments, money still carried the day in the 2008 election cycle. "The 2008 campaign was the costliest in history, [totaling] $5.3 billion in spending by candidates, political parties, and interest groups on both the congressional and presidential races"—"a 27 percent increase over the $4.2 billion spent in the 2004 campaign."[353] The presidential candidates alone spent more than $1 billion,[354] and the money pressure is sure to intensify in 2010 for congressional candidates and in the 2012 presidential election. Much of the money in the past election cycle still came from large donors seeking to purchase influence and access.

This insight—that the source and size of contributions should be the focus of reform—in combination with the other lessons about voter engagement and the infinite potential of the Internet, amounts to a revitalized approach to changing politics as it has been known.[355] The campaign finance agenda should be understood as a key part of a general restructuring of modern campaigns, and now, perhaps, of governance,[356] that creates a new partner in the grassroots through openness and accountability, energizing voters and citizens in a democracy that remains empowered long past election day.[357]

While the "long tail" does not yet wag the dog, it could. Reforms that supercharge smaller donations and require politicians to work with the grassroots—as the new models of public financing do—would democratize campaigns and make politicians more accountable to the many—voters, volunteers, and donors—than they are to the wealthy few.[358] Enhancements in competition for congressional seats would be another welcome change.[359]

The history of BCRA shows that the positive implications of a meaningful shift in incentives for politicians and political institutions can be hoped for, if never fully anticipated. Just as removing soft money from the campaign equation changed the game and brought millions of new donors under the tent, a voluntary program of public funding would likely alter politics in positive ways that even close observers cannot now foresee.[360]

Assumptions about the relationship between money and speech are worth revisiting in light of this new paradigm. Contrary to a popular misconception, in the Supreme Court's landmark campaign finance case, *Buckley v. Valeo*,[361] the Court never equated money with speech. Instead, the Court examined the cost of campaigns and concluded that considerable amounts of money were needed to communicate a candidate's message to voters.

[…]

Or as a reporter for the *Atlantic Monthly* put it: "Obama's campaign is admired by insiders of both parties for its functional beauty—not just admired but gawked at, like some futuristic concept car leaking rocket vapor at an auto show."[364]

While the small-donor revolution has yet to impact congressional politics in a significant way, its impact on presidential campaigning and the national parties encouraged far higher rates of contribution to national politics from average citizens and small donors generally. And with FENA or some similar and comprehensive system of encouragement for small donors, the new online and offline tools and party structures stand ready to make expanded small-donor support for congressional candidates a reality.

As Brooks Jackson put it in his devastating depiction of congressional corruption in the 1980s: "The psychological, even subconscious effect of money is to chill initiatives that donors don't want. As a practical matter, the outcome is the same as if votes had been sold outright. The effect on national policy and well-being is the same."[365]

Voters do connect the dots between the money in politics and failed policies in Washington. An agenda for the new administration should include a codification of the principles that the Obama campaign used to revitalize the 2008 election—principles that support a small-donor model for presidential public financing, and a similar program for members of Congress.

People-powered politics is the way forward, but these new and small donors did not come out to join the party all on their own. In the wake of BCRA, candidates and parties put considerable energy into raising their hard money receipts. The Democratic Party, in particular, focused on grassroots organizing in an effort to rebuild its image as the party of the working class and to make up for years of reliance on soft money.

After more than two decades of partisan fund-raising that pushed the regulatory envelope, campaign finance reform achieved the remarkable: by forcing national parties to wean themselves off of soft money, BCRA sparked a return to the grassroots and, in terms of national politics, handed the political parties and the race for the presidency back to the people.

Notes

1. Simon Rosenberg, Foreword to JEROME ARMSTRONG & MARKOS MOULITSAS, CRASHING THE GATE: NETROOTS, GRASSROOTS, AND THE RISE OF PEOPLE-POWERED POLITICS, at xii (2006).

2. See, e.g., SEAN WILENTZ, THE AGE OF REAGAN: A HISTORY, 1974–2008 (2008).

4. Id.; see also Thomas E. Mann, A Collapse of the Campaign Finance Regime?, FORUM, Vol. 6, Issue 1, Art. 1, at 1–4 (2008); Bradley A. Smith, Obama's Huge Haul Should End This Fight, WASH. POST, Oct. 26, 2008, at B1.

5. Fred Wertheimer, More Money, More Problems, DEMOCRACY J., June 4, 2007, at 77, 78–79.

6. See Smith, supra note 4, at B1.

7. Wertheimer, supra note 5, at 81–82.

8. Bipartisan Campaign Reform Act (BCRA) of 2002, Pub. L. No. 107-155, tit. I, 116 Stat. 81.

9. Seth Gitell, The Democratic Party Suicide Bill, ATLANTIC MONTHLY, July/August 2003, available at http://www.theatlantic.com/doc/200307/gitell.

10. Id.

11. Thomas E. Mann, Money in the 2008 Elections: Bad News or Good?, CHAUTAUQUAN DAILY, July 1, 2008.

12. THE CHANGE ELECTION: MONEY, MOBILIZATION, AND PERSUASION IN THE 2008 FEDERAL ELECTIONS 36 (David B. Magleby ed., 2009).

13. See, e.g., Gitell, supra note 9.

14. See, e.g., PETER FRANCIA ET AL., THE FINANCIERS OF CONGRESSIONAL ELECTIONS 29–41 (2003). By comparing data from the Congressional Donors Survey, the 1996 American National Election Study, and the Census, Peter Francia and his co-authors concluded that the population of partisan donors has long been dominated by white, wealthy, highly-educated men who are middle-aged and older, and generally of

non-Evangelical Protestant religious affiliation. Id. at 29–33. This group has been more readily tapped by Republican candidates. Id. at 37.

15. See David B. Magleby, Rolling in the Dough: The Continued Surge in Individual Contributions to Presidential Candidates and Party Committees, FORUM, Vol. 6, Issue 1, Art. 5, at 10 (2008) ("Contrary to the speculation of some prior to the implementation of BCRA, the soft money ban did not 'short-circuit the efforts . . . to revitalize political parties.'").

16. Norman Ornstein & Anthony Corrado, Jr., Reform That Has Really Paid Off, WASH. POST, Mar. 31, 2007, at B3; see also Magleby, supra note 15, at 1.

17. Magleby, supra note 15, at 1.

18. Press Release, Fed. Election Comm'n, Party Financial Activity Summarized for the 2008 Election Cycle: Party Support for Candidates Increases (May 28, 2009), available at http://www.fec.gov/press2009/05282009Party/20090528Party.shtml. Please note that these figures have been rounded for the reader's convenience.

19. For just one example of the press coverage regarding Clinton's clear early advantage, see Harold Meyerson, How Hillary's Done It—So Far, AM. PROSPECT, Nov. 19, 2007, available at http://www.prospect.org/cs/articles?article=how_hillarys_done_it_so_far.

20. Tim Fernholz, What to Expect When You're Expecting a Majority, AM. PROSPECT, Oct. 1, 2008 (quoting Brian Wolff), available at http://www.prospect.org/cs/articles?article=what_to_ expect_when_youre_expecting_a_majority.

21. Id.

22. See, e.g., ARMSTRONG & MOULITSAS, supra note 1, at 136; Powerpoint Presentation by Micah Sifry, The Making of the President 2.0: How the Process Changed in 2008, http://www.slideshare.net/Msifry/the-making-of-the-president-20-how-the-internet-is-changingthe-political-game-presentation.

345. See MORLEY WINOGRAD & MICHAEL D. HAIS, MILLENNIAL MAKEOVER: MYSPACE, YOUTUBE, AND THE FUTURE OF AMERICAN POLITICS 4 (2008).

346. Zogby International, Zogby Poll: Voters Not Sold on Government Bailout, Sept. 21, 2008, http://www.zogby.com/search/ReadNews.cfm?ID=1555 (last visited Aug. 21, 2009).

347. Lake Research Partners & The Tarrance Group, Memorandum, National Polling on Support for a Proposal to Tackle Big Money in Congressional Elections, Feb. 2009, available at http://www.commoncause.org/atf/cf/%7Bfb3c17e2-cdd1-4df6-92bebd4429893665%7D/POLLIN G%20MEMO%20FEB%202009%20FINAL.PDF.

348. Jeffrey M. Jones, Campaign Financing Appears to Be Non-Issue for Voters, GALLUP, Oct. 30, 2008, http://www.gallup.com/poll/111652/Campaign-Financing-Appears-NonIssue- Voters.aspx (last visited Aug. 21, 2009).

349. Micah Sifry, OFA 2.0 Still a Work in (Hidden) Progress, TECHPRESIDENT, Dec. 15, 2008, http://techpresident.com/node/6612 (last visited Aug. 21, 2009).

350. John Halpin & Ruy Teixeira, Progressivism Goes Mainstream, AM. PROSPECT, Apr. 20, 2009 (citing two new studies that show progressive values characterize the views of more than two-thirds of Americans), available at http://www.prospect.org/cs/articles?article=progressivism_ goes_mainstream.

351. Peter L. Francia & Paul S. Herrnson, The Impact of Public Finance Laws on Fundraising in State Legislative Election, 31 AM. POL. RESEARCH 520, 531 (2003), available at http://apr.sagepub.com/cgi/reprint/31/5/520.

352. Id. The study included data from candidates who participated in partial public funding programs in Minnesota, Wisconsin, and Hawaii. However, such data does not include the time spent by candidates in a hybrid model because of the significant differences between those programs and the hybrid model. The partial funding programs in Minnesota, Wisconsin, and Hawaii function essentially as government subsidies providing candidates with a modest grant without additional matching funds. In contrast, the hybrid models in New York City and the proposed FENA bill provide a significant grant plus matching funds that supercharge small contributions.

353. Jeanne Cummings, 2008 Campaign Costliest in U.S. History, POLITICO, Nov. 5, 2008, available at http://www.politico.com/news/stories/1108/15283.html (last visited Aug. 21, 2009).

354. Kenneth P. Doyle, Record-Shattering $1.8 Billion Cost for '08 Presidential Campaign, FEC Says, in BNA MONEY & POLITICS REPORT (2009); Cummings, supra note 353.

355. See, e.g., Hasen, supra note 198, at 5–6.

356. It appears that the Obama Administration is interested in exploring new modes of public accountability and interaction. See, e.g., Ari Melber, The President's Never-Ending Virtual Town Hall, THE NATION, Mar. 27, 2009, http://www.thenation.com/doc/20090413/melber (last visited Aug. 21, 2009); Presidential Memorandum on Transparency and Open Government, Jan. 21, 2009, available at http://www.whitehouse.gov/the_press_office/Transparency_and_Open_ Government/ (last visited Aug. 21, 2009).

357. For an even broader view of this agenda, see Stuart Comstock-Gay & Joe Goldman, More Than the Vote, AM. PROSPECT, Dec. 12, 2008, available at http://www.prospect.org/ cs/articles?article=more_than_the_vote; Bob Edgar, A 21st Century Agenda for Democratic Renewal, AM. PROSPECT, Dec. 15, 2008, available at http://www.prospect.org/ cs/articles?article=a_21stcentury_agenda_for_democratic_renewal; Larry Marx, A Broader Definition of Democracy, AM. PROSPECT, Dec. 15, 2008, available at http://www.prospect.org/cs/ articles?article=a_broader_definition_of_democracy.

358. For another, related approach, see Schmitt, supra note 3. But see Wertheimer, supra note 5 (demonstrating that public financing can only work in a system of rules).

359. TORRES-SPELLISCY ET AL., supra note 314, at 1–2.

360. A call to focus on small donor reforms is also reflected in recent work by Michael Malbin of CFI. See, e.g., MALBIN, supra note 218, at 11, 14, 21; Michael J. Malbin, Rethinking the Campaign Finance Agenda, FORUM, Vol., 6, Issue 1, Art. 3 (2008), http://www.cfinst. org/books_reports/Participation/Malbin_Rethinking.pdf (last visited Aug. 21, 2009).

361. 424 U.S. 1, 65 n.76 (1976); see also Ciara Torres-Spelliscy, Justices Should Know by Now—Money Is Not Speech, SEATTLE POST-INTELLIGENCER, June 10, 2008, available at http://www.seattlepi.com/opinion/366105_focus08.html (last visited Aug. 21, 2009).

364. Green, supra note 185.

365. JACKSON, supra note 24, at 109.

Periodical and Internet Sources Bibliography

The following articles have been selected to supplement the diverse views presented in this chapter.

All Things Considered, "Watchdog Questions Whether Trump's Payment Is A Campaign Finance Violation," NPR.com, May 3, 2018. https://www.npr.org/2018/05/03/608291878/watchdog-questions-whether-trumps-reimbursement-is-a-campaign-finance-violation.

Jeff Brindle, "Here's How a Small Tax Credit Could Bring Bigger Democracy," The Observer, May 8, 2018. http://observer.com/2018/05/small-tax-credit-could-bring-bigger-democracy/.

Adam Edleman, "Campaign Finance Experts: Trump, Giuliani comments could backfire," NBC News, May 3, 2018. https://www.nbcnews.com/politics/donald-trump/campaign-finance-experts-trump-giuliani-comments-could-backfire-n871091.

Conor Friedersdorf, "The Turn Against Transparency in Campaign Finance," The Atlantic, April 22, 2014. https://www.theatlantic.com/politics/archive/2014/04/charles-krauthammers-shortsighted-turn-against-transparency/361013/.

Brian Fung, "A win for transparency in campaign finance," The Washington Post, July 1, 2014. https://www.washingtonpost.com/news/the-switch/wp/2014/07/01/a-win-for-transparency-in-campaign-finance/?noredirect=on&utm_term=.a741e83dd8e9.

Richard L. Hasen, "Rudy Giuliani May Have Just Implicated President Trump In Serious Campaign Finance Violations," Slate.com, May 3, 2018. https://slate.com/news-and-politics/2018/05/rudy-giuliani-may-have-just-implicated-president-trump-in-serious-campaign-finance-violations.html.

Arn Pearson, "Trump May Face Heat for Campaign Finance Crimes," PR Watch.org, April 18, 2018. https://www.prwatch.org/news/2018/04/13342/trump-may-face-heat-campaign-finance-crimes.

Ann M. Ravel, "States can bring political 'dark money' into the light," LA Times, July 20, 2016. http://www.latimes.com/opinion/op-ed/

la-oe-ravel-dark-money-campaign-spending-20160718-snap-story.html.

Tim Roemer & Zach Wamp, "John McCain's Warning about dark money is real. Stop campaign finance corruption," USA Today, May 8, 2018. https://www.usatoday.com/story/opinion/2018/05/08/sen-mccain-dark-money-campaign-finance-column/585109002/.

Ruth Serven, "At UVa, Feingold bemoans state of politics," Daily Progress, April 23, 2018. http://www.dailyprogress.com/news/local/at-uva-feingold-bemoans-state-of-politics/article_07735e78-4746-11e8-947b-bb3abe7bba6b.html.

Dimitry Shapiro, Arthur Zillante, "Contribution Limits and Transparency in a Campaign Finance Experiment," Wiley Online Library, April 28, 2017. https://onlinelibrary.wiley.com/doi/full/10.1002/soej.12220.

Iris Zhang, Chisun Lee, "States Lead the Way in Enforcing Campaign Finance Transparency," The Brennan Center, May 12, 2017. https://www.brennancenter.org/blog/states-lead-way-enforcing-campaign-finance-transparency.

For Further Discussion

Chapter 1

1. Why is it important that there are fewer races with unopposed incumbents?
2. What are the difficulties behind expanding access to politics in other countries?
3. What led to Congress accidentally making soft money donations illegal in the 1970s?

Chapter 2

1. Is it accurate to claim that candidates do not coordinate with *Super PACs*? Why or why not?
2. Should the US have stricter regulations on campaign finance? Why or why not?
3. Why is there an important correlation between tax changes and charitable giving?

Chapter 3

1. What are the ways in which corporations and labor organizations can get around the laws regulating how they can support a candidate during federal elections?
2. What influences major reforms in campaign finance and why?
3. Why is it more likely for donors to arrange meetings with high-level governmental officials?

Chapter 4

1. Has the *Citizens United* decision helped or hindered federal elections in the US?
2. How can voter turnout be expanded to match up with the rising levels of election spending?
3. What were the implied reasons behind the Sanders campaign's decision to claim the Clinton campaign violated campaign finance law?

Organizations to Contact

The editors have compiled the following list of organizations concerned with the issues debated in this book. The descriptions are derived from materials provided by the organizations. All have publications or information available for interested readers. The list was compiled on the date of publication of the present volume; the information provided here may change. Be aware that many organizations take several weeks or longer to respond to inquiries, so allow as much time as possible.

Association of Fundraising Professionals

4300 Wilson Blvd, Suite 300, Arlington, VA 22203
(703) 684-0410
email: tmclaughlin@afpnet.org
website: www.afpnet.org

The Association of Fundraising Professionals (AFP) represents more than 30,000 members in over 230 chapters throughout the world, working to advance philanthropy through advocacy, research, education and certification programs.

Brennan Center for Justice

120 Broadway, Suite 1750, New York, NY 10271
(646) 292-8310
email: brennancenter@nyu.edu
website: www.brenancenter.org

The Brennan Center for Justice at NYU School of Law is a nonpartisan law and policy institute that works to reform, revitalize—and when necessary, defend—systems of democracy and justice. The Brennan Center focuses on voting rights, campaign finance reform, ending mass incarceration, and preserving liberties while also maintaining our national security.

The Campaign Finance Institute

1776 Eye St NY, Washington, D.C. 20006
(202) 969-8890
email: info@cfinst.org
website: www.cfinst.org

Founded in 1999, CFI has successfully established its reputation as the nation's pre-eminent think tank for campaign finance policy. Written to meet peer-reviewed standards, CFI's original work is published in academic journals as well as in forms regularly used by the media and policy makers.

Cato Institute

1000 Massachusetts Ave NW, Washington, D.C. 20001
(202) 842-0200
email: pr@cato.org
website: www.cato.org

The Cato Institute is a public policy research organization—a think tank—dedicated to the principles of individual liberty, limited government, free markets and peace. Its scholars and analysts conduct independent, nonpartisan research on a wide range of policy issues.

The Center for Responsive Politics

1300 L St NW, Suite 200, Washington, D.C. 20005
(202) 857-0044
email: commercial@crp.org
website: www.opensecrets.org

The Center for Responsive Politics pursues their mission largely through their award-winning website, OpenSecrets.org, which is the most comprehensive resource for federal campaign contributions, lobbying data and analysis available anywhere. And for other organizations and news media, the Center's exclusive data powers their online features tracking money in politics—counting cash to make change.

Demos

80 Broad Street, 4th Floor, New York, NY 10004
(212) 633.1405
email: info@demos.org
website: www.demos.org

Demos is a public policy organization working for all Americans have an equal say in their democracy and an equal chance in their economy. Demos works to reduce both political and economic inequality, deploying original research, advocacy, litigation, and strategic communications to create the America the people deserve.

EveryVoice

1211 Connecticut Ave NW, Suite 600, Washington, D.C. 20036
(202) 640-5600
email: info@everyvoice.org
website: everyvoice.org

Every Voice Action builds the political power necessary to create a democracy where your political influence isn't determined by your net worth and every voice is heard. They run and win campaigns that support champions of reform at the federal and state level and demonstrate that there is a political cost to opposing reform, by running hard-hitting campaigns opposing candidates that support the status quo.

International Foundation for Electoral Systems

2011 Crystal Drive, 10th Floor, Arlington, VA 22202
(202) 350-6700
email: info@ifes.org
website: www.ifes.org

As a global leader in democracy promotion, the International Foundation for Electoral Systems (IFES) engages with critical issues in democracy, governance and elections around the world. From programming aimed at ensuring electoral integrity and accountability to efforts to empower underrepresented populations, such as persons with disabilities, women and youth, to participate in electoral and political processes, IFES is at the forefront of innovative work to provide citizens around the world with the fundamental human right to have a say in how they are governed.

International Institute for Democracy and Electoral Assistance

Strömsborg, SE-103 34, Stockholm, Sweden
+46 8 689 37 00
email: info@idea.int
website: www.idea.int

The organization is governed by its Statutes, the latest of which entered ino force November 2008. Membership in International IDEA is open to governments which demonstrate, by example in their own state, their commitment to the rule of law, human rights, the basic principles of democratic pluralism and strengthening democracy.

National Conference of State Legislatures

444 North Capitol Street NW, Suite 515, Washington, D.C. 20001
(202) 624-5400
email: ncslnet-admin@ncsl.org
website: www.ncsl.org

Since 1975, NCSL has been the champion of state legislatures, helping states remain strong and independent by giving them the tools, information and resources to craft the best solutions to difficult problems. The NCSL has fought against unwarranted actions in Congress and saved states more than $1 billion.

Organisation for Economic Co-operation and Development, Washington Center

1776 I Street, NW, Suite 450, Washington, D.C. 2006
(202) 785-6323
email: Washington.contact@oecd.org
website: www.oecd.org

The OECD provides a forum in which governments can work together to share experiences and seek solutions to common problems. They work with governments to understand what drives economic, social and environmental change and analyse and compare data to predict future trends.

Bibliography of Books

Robert G. Boatright. *Routledge Handbook of Primary Elections.* Abingdon, United Kingdom: Routledge, 2018

Sayu Bhojwani. *People Like Us: The New Wave of Candidates Knocking at Democracy's Door.* New York, NY: The New Press, 2018

Jeffrey D. Clements. *Corporations Are Not People: Reclaiming Democracy from Big Money and Global Corporations.* Oakland, CA: Berrett-Koehler Publishers, 2014

Richard Collins, David Skover. *When Money Speaks: The McCutcheon Decision, Campaign Finance Laws, and the First Amendment.* Oak Park, IL: Top Five Books, LLC, 2014

Andrew Dowdie, Scott Limbocker, Patrick A. Stewart, Karen Sebold, Joshua L Mitchell. *The Political Geography of Campaign Finance: Fundraising and Contribution.* New York, NY: Springer Publishing, 2012

Erika Franklin Fowler et al. *Political Advertising in the United States.* Abingdon, United Kingdom: Routledge, 2018

Richard L. Hasen. *Plutocrats United: Campaign Money, the Supreme Court, and the Distortion of American Elections.* New Haven, CT: Yale University Press, 2016

Lawrence Lessig. *Republic, Lost: Version 2.0.* New York City, NY: Hachette Book Group, 2016

Jane Mayer. *Dark Money: The Hidden History of the Billionaires Behind the Rise of the Radical Right.* New York, NY: Anchor, 2017

Jane Mayer. *Summary of Dark Money.* New York, NY: Penguin Random House, 2017

Mary Jo McGowan Shepherd. *Campaign Finance Complexity: Before Campaigning Retain an Attorney.* Lanham, MD: Lexington Books, 2018

Robert E Mutch, *Buying the Vote: A History of Campaign Finance Reform.* Oxford, United Kingdom: Oxford University Press, 2016

Robert E Mutch. *Campaign Finance—What Everyone Needs to Know.* Oxford, United Kingdom: Oxford University Press, 2016

Costas Panagopoulos. *Congressional Challengers: Candidate Quality in US Elections to Congress.* Abingdon, United Kingdom: Routledge, 2018

Robert Post. *Citizens Divided.* Cambridge, MA: Harvard University Press, 2014

Rodney A Smith. *Money, Power, and Elections: How Campaign Finance Reform Subverts American Democracy.* Baton Rouge, LA: Louisiana State University Press, 2006

Frank J. Sorauf. *Inside Campaign Finance: Myths and Realities.* New Haven, CT: Yale University Press, 1992

Zephyr Teachout. *Corruption in America: From Benjamin Franklin's Snuff Box to Citizens United.* Cambridge, MA: Harvard University Press, 2016

Stephen J. Wayne. *Is This Any Way to Run a Democratic Election?* Abingdon, United Kingdom: Routledge, 2018

Index

Super Political Action Committees (Super PACs), 62, 66, 84–90, 92, 96, 106, 108, 109, 111–113, 114, 115–116, 128, 135, 137–149, 154, 161, 165, 167

T

Taft-Hartley Act, 114
Tea Party, 113, 116
third party, 31, 45, 47, 82, 124, 139
Thompson, Fred, 89
Tillman Act, 14, 114
Toobin, Jeffrey, 99
two-party system, 45, 46

U

Udall, Mark, 145
US Constitution, 7, 15, 19, 20, 21–28, 30, 31, 45, 46, 48, 61, 76–78, 81, 86, 96–97, 114, 138, 146, 150, 163, 177

V

Van Hollen, Chris, 145
van Kessel, Patrick, 160–165
voter registration, 75–76, 96, 155

W

Waldman, Paul, 98–104
Wallace, George, 45, 46–48
Wang, Marian, 108–116
Warren, Elizabeth, 18
Washington, George, 71
Washington Post (WP), 128, 156, 157, 159,

Watergate Scandal, 15, 109, 113, 135, 145, 150
wealthy donors, 59, 65, 109, 128, 172, 173, 175, 178
Wertheimer, Fred, 110, 163
Wihbey, John, 127–131
Wolff, Brian, 175
Wolkoff, Adam, 18, 19–28
women running for office, 35–36